THROUGH JASPER'S EYES

MY WEEKEND ON DEATH ROW

JOHN LIPSCOMB

ELECTIO PUBLISHING
first century principles.
a twenty-first century approach.

Through Jasper's Eyes: My Weekend on Death Row
By John Lipscomb

Copyright 2018 by John Lipscomb. All rights reserved.
Cover Design by eLectio Publishing

ISBN-13: 978-1-63213-526-1

Published by eLectio Publishing, LLC

Little Elm, Texas

http://www.eLectioPublishing.com

5 4 3 2 1 eLP 22 21 20 19 18

Printed in the United States of America.

The eLectio Publishing creative team is comprised of: Kaitlyn Campbell, Emily Certain, Lori Draft, Jim Eccles, Sheldon James, and Christine LePorte.

Publisher's Note

The publisher does not have any control over and does not assume any responsibility for author or third-party websites or their content.

CONTENTS

IN MEMORY

Charles J. Cella

David Lee Gardner, Jr.

Carolyn Carol Borders Danforth

Judy Ann Lipscomb McCaffrey

Judy Zisk Lincoff

Bobby Ray Reiss

Marcus Wellington Smith

Each and every one of these individuals helped form who I am today. And sadly, each one of these individuals passed away while I was writing *Through Jasper's Eyes.*

Certainly my life is not as full and the world as a whole is not as bright without Uncle Charles, David, Carol, Judy, Judy, Bobby, and Marcus in it.

I wish to thank their families and friends for sharing their lives with me, and I hope this book is a fitting tribute to some incredible souls.

May you rest in peace.

—Johnny

Chapter 1
The Burning Bush

JANUARY 5, 1999 started much the same as the days before.

I woke up on my couch. A nest of empty beer cans surrounded me. The ashtray was full to overflowing. It was cold outside the house, one of the coldest days on record. Just to get my mind and shaking body moving toward some sense of equilibrium, I drank a beer, wretched, and then drank two more.

I didn't know why I promised her I would go to this appointment.

But I respected her, which was enough to get me up off the couch to pull on my coat and drag myself out into air that was so cold, it hurt my face and lungs to breathe it in. I tossed three beers into my dented and rust-spotted red truck. In the bed were tools for installing the DogWatch hidden dog fences I sold.

Two beers were for the ride there, and one was for the ride back with a stop for a couple more cases and maybe some wine or, better yet, vodka in honor of Mom.

The engine was slow to turn over. In the footwell of the passenger seat was a pile of beer cans, crushed and tossed aside. The ashtray was overflowing. I wound the window down and dumped it out on the side of the street and pulled away.

I opened a beer and took a long sip then set it between my thighs. The heat started to blow through the vents, but my body couldn't stop shaking. I took another pull from the beer.

Edgewood, the rehabilitation center where she'd set up the appointment, wasn't far. Twenty minutes on a normal day, but in the cold, and fearful of speeding, I took an extra five minutes to get there.

The tools in the bed rattled as I pulled into the parking area. I stepped out of the truck and killed the last of the second beer, crumpled the can, and tossed it into the truck. It landed next to the last full beer. I trudged across the ice-covered parking lot toward the entry.

I walked through the automatic doors, and a wave of hot air blew down on me from a vent as I entered the building. Then there was noise. My eyes followed the sound to a large room where some twenty to thirty people were laughing, hugging, and smiling. Each was talking loudly to be heard above the din.

I had no idea what in the world that was all about.

There was a bathroom a few feet away. I ducked into it and splashed warm water over my face. My breath was stale and tasted of beer and cigarettes. Staring into the mirror, I didn't recognize the old man, many years my senior, with black sunken eyes who looked back at me. He was bloated, shaking, and sweaty, and his skin and the whites of his eyes were sallow and jaundiced.

I dried my hands with a paper towel. *This is horrible,* I thought to myself. *I want out.* My body already needed more alcohol. The pain of that need was sharp and ached into my chest and bones. The tremors were so bad that I resembled a paint can shaker in a hardware store.

The list of my issues was endless: three DWIs, driver's license revoked for a year, car repossessed, home close to foreclosure, three years of unfiled and unpaid tax returns, business close to being closed due to unpaid accounts, terrible health with gout and high blood pressure. I had chased everyone out of my life, including family. My wife was long gone, and, worst of all, my children were out of my life.

And among all my many fears, the scariest was the threat of going to jail. It was the fear of losing control, the fear of losing my material possessions, of losing the affluent life I grandiosely believed I had, and the deep, penetrating fear of the unknown of prison. According to my lawyer, prison was possible.

Donnie was a mafia lawyer, a powerful guy, and he had also been Mom's lawyer for many years. When I came to him after my second DWI, he said he wouldn't charge me because he'd made so much money off Mom. Then, after my third DWI, he said, "I don't know if there's anything I can do for you at this point. There is a distinct possibility you will go to prison."

"Country club prison?" I asked.

"No. Real prison."

He told me to start going to AA, to do anything I could to show I was contrite, and to seek help to get the judge off my back. I went to a couple of meetings but kept drinking. In the end, the judge ordered me to do community service and attend MADD meetings, and he took my license for a year. The last thing the judge said was if I didn't get my act together, he'd have no regrets sending me to prison for a good long time.

And yet I was still driving around town drinking with a pile of empty beer cans in the cab of my pickup truck. This is the insanity of the disease.

I walked down the hall to where a large sign said INTAKE. There was a window, and a woman slid the glass open.

"I'm Johnny Lipscomb. I have an appointment."

"Take a seat."

In a moment, a middle-aged doctor with salt-and-pepper hair wearing a white coat greeted me and guided me to an exam room.

He leaned back in his chair. "Why are you here?" His eyes narrowed. He looked me up and down.

"A friend is worried about me, so I said I would come and get checked out."

"What is she worried about?"

"My drinking."

"Are you worried about your drinking?"

"I suppose."

"Have you been drinking already today?"

"No," I lied.

He looked at me for a moment. Then he asked me to roll my sleeve up so he could take my blood pressure.

"Your blood pressure's sky high. Did you know that?"

"No," I lied, again.

He checked my pulse.

"Your pulse is racing. If you don't do something about this, you're going to have a stroke or a heart attack soon."

The pain of no alcohol became panic as I realized my beer, my last beer, would freeze in the truck if I stayed much longer.

"How soon? Today?"

"Soon."

He handed me a three-page form and asked me to fill it out. There were twenty questions—it was the Johns Hopkins Twenty Questions test to determine if you are an alcoholic or not, and I answered yes to all twenty.

Probably the first test in my life on which I got a perfect score.

The doctor looked at my answers for a moment and then said to me, "I'm probably not telling you anything you don't already know, but you have a serious drinking problem. If you don't do something about it, you won't live much longer."

His tone was flat. There was no emotion behind his words. His attitude and bearing was that of an expert stating an obvious fact.

My brain and body screamed for me to run away. *Get to that beer before it's too late and then go to the store and drink this away.* I felt sicker than when I had walked in, and my shaking intensified to near convulsing as my body warmed with anxiety, embarrassment, and fear.

I squeezed my hands so tightly that my fingers turned white. "Okay," I said.

"We need to check you in."

"When? Tomorrow? A week?"

"Right now, Mr. Lipscomb. I can't compel you to enter our program—you must agree to it—but if you walk out that door, I'm afraid I'll never see you again."

"Can you stop the shaking?" My body hadn't stopped shaking for weeks, and I'd had the sweats so bad that my sheets were stained yellow.

"We can help."

"I'll do anything if you can just stop the shaking."

An hour later, I was in a hospital room in the basement, detoxing. The pain was unreal. The shaking wouldn't stop, even though the doctor gave me Librium, and the drug made me feel even hazier, which was probably a good thing. I was tired, but I couldn't sleep. Every muscle in my body twitched, I was damp with sweat, and my stomach was cramping.

If this doesn't get better soon, I'm out of here.

All I wanted was to leave, but I was too afraid to get up and walk out. I clenched the under-sheet with my hands and held on for dear life. I looked at the clock. It said 1:32. I clenched the sheet harder. I squeezed my eyes shut, and it felt as if my entire body was pulsing. My muscles wouldn't stop trembling, and yet I was so damn tired.

For God's sake, why can't I sleep?

I looked back at the clock, and it was 1:34. I had no idea if it was morning or afternoon.

Adding to the stress was my roommate. His name was JR, and he was going through drug detox. He was in his mid-thirties, tall and lean, with a wisp of straight black hair that hung across his eyes. He pushed it back in a tic-like motion as he paced back and forth, muttering to himself. The muttering reminded me of the woman, Lizzy, who was more of a mother to me than Mom. She used to work around the kitchen, talking to herself in a low, insistent hum.

"What are you here for?" I asked.

He turned and looked at me but kept pacing and muttering. I asked again, and he still didn't respond. I tried once more.

"I work, I should say I *worked*, because there's no way that guy's ever gonna have me back. So I worked for a veterinarian. I love animals, and that's something that isn't germane to why I'm here, but it's very germane to who I am, but maybe, tangentially, it *is* germane to why I'm here, which is because I found out that the doggie downers we had at the clinic are really great to shoot up, but now, apparently, they are absolutely impossible to come down from, so if I stop walking or have to answer another question too soon, I'm not going to do it because the only thing that helps with this absolutely miserable pain is to keep moving, because if I could sleep, I would, but every muscle in my body is twitching like it's connected to some sort of electrode—"

"Me too," I said.

"You too, what?"

"My muscles twitch too."

"Doggie downers?"

"No, alcohol."

"Got it. Can't stop, can't talk."

He went back to pacing. I shut my eyes tight.

Every hour, a nurse came to take my vitals. There was worry in her eyes, and I wondered if they'd just send me to a hospital ICU unit like Mom.

Every so often, a doctor came into the room. He asked how I was doing and then why I was there.

"A friend asked me to do it."

"Why did she ask you to come here?"

My body was bloated, sweaty, and yellow, and the DTs caused me to rattle. "Dunno. I drink too much."

"Why did you hear her when you heard no one else?"

"Out of respect, I guess. She feels safe, like a mother."

He leaned back. "Yeah?"

"Yeah. So I kept my word."

He thought for a moment. "Would you say you're an alcoholic?"

"Yes."

"Okay, then you're in the right place."

After he left, I lay flat in bed, shaking and sweating, swearing that if it didn't get better, I was going to walk out of here and buy a bottle of wine and a case of beer.

I was exhausted, but I still couldn't sleep. The Librium made consciousness distant, like going down a tube through a cloud. My body ached, and my muscles twitched. I couldn't find a position where I was not in pain. I couldn't stop shaking. I held on to the bed for dear life.

Consciousness faded, and I lapsed into a state that was neither awake nor asleep but was restful.

"Mr. Lipscomb, time to take your vitals."

The soft voice was unwelcome.

"How are you?" She wrapped the blood pressure cuff around my arm and started pumping it.

"Not great. If things don't get better, then I'm out of here."

"There's an AA meeting this morning you could go to."

"Alcoholics Anonymous?"

"Uh-huh." She unwrapped the cuff. "Your blood pressure is still very high." She lifted my wrist to take my pulse.

"I feel horrible."

"Well, we aren't allowed to give you any stimulants—that includes coffee—but if you go to the meeting, they have coffee and maybe a donut or a muffin, something like that."

"I think I'll try."

An hour later, I walked upstairs in a bathrobe and hospital socks and went into the room I'd passed the day before. There were the same twenty or thirty people, and they were laughing and hugging each other. I walked toward the table that held the coffee and donuts. As I passed small groups of two or three people, they smiled and said welcome.

A guy said, "One day at a time" and patted me on the back.

I overheard a woman say, "The definition of an alcoholic is an egomaniac with an inferiority complex." The two men beside her smiled and looked down at their shoes. They'd heard that one a lot.

Another man said, "I'm glad to see you made it today."

My hands shook so much I had difficulty holding a Styrofoam cup steady while pumping the coffee dispenser. My hands moved like they were ninety-nine years old. An older woman in her mid-fifties said, "Let me do that."

I looked at her. She had untamed, gray-streaked hair and smiling brown eyes.

"You're a Lipscomb, aren't you?"

"How did you know that?"

"I waited on your daddy at the club for many years."

She handed me the cup of coffee. I turned and looked around the room. Almost everyone was smiling. There were a couple of people who, like me, seemed lost and confused.

A voice, deeper this time, from behind me asked, "Are you Johnny Lipscomb?"

I turned, and there was a tall, lean man in his forties with close-cropped hair.

"I'm sorry. I recognize you, but I can't place where or why."

"That's okay. It's been a while. I'm Dave. You used to buy flowers from me, both you and your dad. Your dad still does."

"You're a florist. Right, I'm sorry."

"It's okay. I'm glad you made it here. It gets better, I promise."

We all sat in folding chairs, and the meeting began with "God, grant me the serenity to accept the things I cannot change, the courage to change the things I can, and the wisdom to know the difference."

After a few announcements, the leader—a middle-aged woman—asked if there were any newcomers. I raised my hand with three or four others.

People turned to us and said, "Welcome."

Then a woman stood to speak. She looked tired but confident, comfortable.

"Hello, my name is Alice, and I'm an alcoholic."

Everyone responded, "Hi, Alice."

"When Nancy asked me to speak, I wasn't sure what to say. Like most of you, the day my life started falling apart was the day I took my first drink.

"It took some time for me to recognize it, but I think when I was in my mid-twenties I knew I was an alcoholic. For some reason, it wasn't until I was forty-five that I finally got sober"—a number of people in the room smiled—"For twenty years I knew I was killing myself with alcohol.

"Why did it take so long for me to stop? I don't know the answer to that."

Around the room, heads nodded.

"It's as if half of me knew I had to stop, but the other half that wanted to keep drinking held more power over me. It wasn't until I knew, I mean, really knew that death was coming."

I saw myself in her story.

She finished, and everyone said, "Thanks, Alice."

A few more people shared their stories, and then the group stood in a circle holding hands. I stayed in my seat, but no one seemed to notice.

Together, they prayed:

> *Our father, which art in heaven,*
> *Hallowed be thy name.*
> *Thy kingdom come.*
> *Thy will be done on earth,*
> *As it is in heaven.*
> *Give us this day our daily bread.*
> *And forgive us our trespasses,*
> *As we forgive them that trespass against us.*
> *And lead us not into temptation,*
> *But deliver us from evil.*
> *For thine is the kingdom,*

The power, and the glory,
Forever and ever.
Amen.

Then they all lifted and dropped their hands as they said, "Keep coming back. It works if you work it!"

It had been a long time since I was in a church, and I didn't remember that last line. Oh well.

A few people introduced themselves and said they were glad I came. One man said, "Easy does it." Another said, "One day at a time."

They put on their coats and walked out into the world sober, working to become better people. I walked back downstairs to my room. JR was relentless in his pacing and muttering. My body was in pain and shuddering so hard I felt like it would shatter.

"If this doesn't get better soon, I'm leaving," I murmured. But I saw a way forward. I even saw what it looked like to reach the other side.

The rest of the day was discussions with a counselor, a group meeting of inpatients with JR pacing behind and around us, and lots of time in bed holding on for dear life. The twitching in my muscles, the stomach cramps, and the Librium haze created a sense of confusion. I felt overwhelmed by the misery of it all.

"Can I make a call?" I asked a nurse.

"Who to?"

"My dad. Please, I need to speak to my dad."

She frowned a little but said yes.

"Dad, I can't do this. I gotta get out of here."

"Johnny, please. I love you so much. Please don't."

"Dad, I'm walking out of here. You have to listen to me. I can't take it anymore."

"You're stronger than you think."

"No, I'm not."

"You are, Johnny. Your mother wasn't, but I swear to you, you are."

I decided to stay, but I repeated to myself, "If it doesn't get any better, I'm getting a drink."

It was Friday, January 8. I had been in rehab for four days.

"Johnny," one of the counselors said, "your insurance won't cover your stay here past tomorrow. I can't overemphasize how important it is for you to be here for thirty days. Can you afford to stay here?"

I didn't have to consider the question too long. Town & Country Shoes, the source of Dad's wealth, had filed for bankruptcy twenty years ago. Mom came from one of the wealthiest families in St. Louis, but she was a tragic, helpless drunk. Dale, my stepfather, and others preyed on her and left little for my brother, sister, and me. What the vultures who picked at Mom's remains didn't take was used for college and for providing us a modest start in life.

It was quite a fall. I grew up with a nanny, private planes, grandparents with homes on Millionaire's Row in St. Louis, private schools, fancy sleepover camps, and all the rest, but now I was broke with a flagging business selling and installing hidden dog fences.

"No, I can't afford it."

"I'm sorry, but we have to let you go home tomorrow. Is there anyone you can call?"

"No."

"Okay, listen, you aren't fully cooked yet."

"Fully cooked?"

"You won't make it out there on your own. You'll start drinking again, only this time you may not find your way back here."

"Okay."

"You need an outpatient program."

I thought, for the hundredth time, if the shaking, pain, and craving didn't get better, I was going to drink.

"Where should I go?"

"We recommend a program called Exodus. They're your best bet. Can you do it?"

"I think so."

The next day, in the early evening, I walked out the front door for the first time in five days. This was the longest I'd gone without a drink in two decades. I was shaking, on Librium, in pain, clueless, scared, and alone.

The temperature was near zero. The door to my truck squeaked as it opened. Inside, there were nine or ten beer cans scattered on the seat and floor. The lone unopened beer rested against the seatback where I'd left it. It looked as if it had been waiting for me. I threw it as hard and far as I could across the parking lot.

The engine was sluggish to turn over, but it did, and within a half hour, I was home.

The house was like a time capsule of my final days. The tableau was what a person finding my corpse would have seen.

The angry red light on the answering machine blinked. There were beer cans all over the kitchen and living room. Ashtrays were full to overflowing. The plate from my final meal four weeks ago and a few other dishes sat in the sink with food remnants crusted on them. The trash reeked.

I moved through the house looking at it all, almost like Scrooge in *A Christmas Carol* witnessing the wake of his death. I was overwhelmed and fell to my knees. Sobbing, I buried my face in my hands.

Six days before, I would have drunk myself into oblivion, but my best friend, alcohol, was gone. Among the papers the counselor had given me was a list of AA meetings. I found one that started in an hour. I washed my face, brushed my teeth, and did what I could to pull myself together.

I headed down the road in the freezing cold in my truck, and after about twenty minutes, I pulled up in front of a Methodist church. It was quiet, and there were no lights. I went to the large wooden doors leading to the nave, but they were locked. I walked around the side to a small door, but it was locked, too. I saw a note in the door window—the meeting was canceled. I walked back to my truck and shouted out, "Help me! I'm trying!"

I didn't sleep well, but I hauled myself out of bed. I was trembling and in pain, and the deep, persistent compulsion to drink had not left.

It was Sunday, so I put on a Brooks Brothers wool suit, nice shoes, and a tie.

I looked at my yellow, bloated body and florid face in the mirror. Tears flowed without restraint. *I'll give this another day or two, but if it doesn't get better, I don't care. I'm going back to what works.*

I decided to go back to the Edgewood AA meeting where I at least knew a few faces.

"Johnny, glad to see you here." An older man with gray hair and a ruddy Irish face smiled and held his hand out toward me. "I haven't seen you in years, Johnny. I'm a friend of your dad's."

My eyes were blank as I looked at him.

"Your dad and I sold shoes together." His shoulders tilted up.

"How are you?"

"Good. Say hello to your father for me." He patted me on the back and walked away.

I poured coffee into a Styrofoam cup and sat quietly in a chair toward the back of the room.

###

Monday, January 11, 1999, I walked into Exodus. They were expecting me. A tall man with dark hair wearing khakis and a dress shirt met me at the front desk.

"I recognize you," he said.

"You do?"

"Yeah, you came in a few weeks ago, but I'm not surprised you don't remember."

"Why?"

"You were speaking Chinese."

He led me down a hallway into a room that looked like a combination of an exam room and therapist's office.

"You'll be working with Barbara. She's a counselor, and she should be here any moment. Good luck, Johnny."

He closed the door, and a few minutes later a tiny, middle-aged woman walked in. She had black hair, crinkled eyes, and was composed of spit and confidence. She asked me to tell her my story, which I did. She asked many more questions, and I did my best to be truthful.

"I think we can help you."

"I hope so."

"We run a twelve-week program, two nights per week. The rest of the time we want you to go to as many AA meetings as you can — ninety meetings in ninety days is what I recommend. Think of them as your lifeboat until we can get to the root of your drinking. Okay?"

I thought that many meetings was ridiculous, but I said, "Okay."

"During the evenings, we do a lot of work in-group, but you'll also spend time with me one-on-one. One of the nights, Thursday, there's time for family to come in. Usually, that would be a wife, kids maybe, but given your situation, could you find someone?"

I nodded.

When we finished, I went home and called Dad.

"Johnny, I told you, I'm here when you need me. I love you. Of course I'll do it."

Of the twelve sessions, Dad made it to eleven.

The first few weeks were okay. I went to an AA meeting each day and Exodus two nights per week. I listened and shared when I felt like I could, but I wasn't leaping out of my seat to share with the group.

Barbara knew everything there was to know about the disease of addiction and had something new for me to try every session. The problem was, I didn't internalize any of it or engage. Instead of following the program, I tried to manipulate it and avoid what felt difficult.

And yet I came to her each session and told her I was barely holding on.

After about five weeks, Barbara became fed up with offering guidance I didn't listen to.

"Barbara, I'm miserable. If something doesn't change soon, I'm not going to keep hanging on."

Barbara ran her fingers through her hair and then put both hands in her lap.

"Johnny, this is a simple program for complicated people. If everyone who wanted to get sober would just show up, shut up, listen, help others, and do what people who know what they're doing suggest, there would be more sober alcoholics. The program isn't failing you—you're failing the program."

"What do you mean? I've been doing everything—"

"No, you haven't. You've been putting conditions on what you will or won't do to save your own life, to stay sober. You're unwilling to do this or that, many of the things you need to do. What you're trying to do is personalize your program so that it's Johnny's Anonymous.

"Johnny, this is a family disease. Think of your mother. Think of the effect her drinking had on you, your sister and brother, your father—on everyone around her. Think of how she never engaged with the cure, only the problem. And think of the effect your drinking has had on you, your family, your ex-wife, and the decision to marry her, but most importantly, how your drinking has affected your children."

"They won't see or talk to me."

"Your own children don't want to have a relationship with you, Johnny. I think you even said that they escaped you the way you wished you could have escaped your mother."

Tears welled and then ran down my cheeks, which were warmed by shame.

"I've become my mother."

"No, not yet. You're still trying to get better."

I put my face in my hands.

"Johnny, you need to forgive your mother and let go of what she's done to you."

"She's dead," I said through my fingers.

"I want you to write a letter to her."

"Why would I do that? I hated her, and she was a complete wreck and probably why I'm here right now."

"Shut up and go do it."

I drove home and sat down with a pad of paper. I stared at it for an hour. I threw it across the room. I picked it up and sat down again. I stared at it. Then I remembered a bit of writing advice a friend once shared: *Start with just one true sentence.*

I wrote:

> *As of this date, you have been gone from my life for eighteen years. I feel like I have never had a mother and honestly remember very little of you. I am filled with so many what-ifs. Maybe I should start at the beginning.*

One sentence flowed into the next, and for two hours I hovered over that pad of paper, sobbing. I spoke with Mom in a way I never had or could have. I felt each resentment like a cancer, its black tendrils penetrating deep into the tissue of my heart and psyche. As my words touched each of these lesions, they burned and throbbed. They awoke a child's yearning for a mother's embrace, a mother's love. They awoke a need to understand why she didn't love me enough. Was I unlovable?

My body shivered, not just from the raw sweat of withdrawal, but from rage, anguish, and loss.

The next evening, I brought the letter to Barbara.

She was quiet as she read. "This is good, Johnny. It reads true."

"Thank you."

"Now I want you to read it to the group."

"What?"

"Read it to the group."

"Tonight?"

"Yes."

"No way."

"Johnny, I'm small, but I'm tough. Let go and stop placing conditions on how you stop killing yourself. Read this letter tonight."

And so, an hour later, I stood before about twenty people. Tears fell down my cheeks even before I started. I struggled to keep my body still and my voice steady, but it was no good. I melted.

Mom, up to age nine I have very few memories of you. I have fond memories of Lizzy and, in all honesty, I consider Lizzy to be my mother. I remember walking with her down the lane, spending most of my time with her, and feeling safe in her presence. She would have laid down her life for me, and I know she loved me. "As much as a kitten loves cream," she used to say. I remember, too, when I was a boy, she would say, "John David, I knew you were coming home to me because I could see your soft blond hair bouncing from the woods and up the yard."

I have no memory of you saying such things.

What I remember is after Dad and you told us the two of you were divorcing, you took us to Florida. The staff at the hotel carried you up to our room because you were so drunk. And I remember Dad tying you up in the pantry when he came by the house after we got back because you were in a drunken rage and threw your body onto his car. He told me to untie you once he left.

You were sent away.

Then you came back, and we went through the custody fight. How could you put us through that terrifying ordeal and then separate us? On top of that, you married Dale, who was verbally abusive to all of us and physically abusive to Joshua.

Most of my memories of you are from age fifteen on, and they are not pretty. Didn't you ever wonder why I didn't bring friends around? Not one friend, including Margaret. Would you even know who she is and what she meant to me?

My lasting memory of you is you lying passed out on the couch in your urine-soaked nightgown day after day, night after night, with cigarette burns in the carpet below you.

I remember thinking I was never going to be like you. The many ambulances in the driveway, the trips to the hospital because you fell. Being rushed out of a restaurant in front of so many people who knew our family, and the only time I remember you driving, you got pulled over for your drunken driving.

At age twenty-two, I received a call that you were in a coma. All the tubes coming out of you, yellow-skinned and bloated—that is the memory I am left with. None of us shed a tear at that moment or at your funeral, where there were only five people in attendance.

I am mad, Mom, angry and full of resentment. How could you? I have grown close to most of my girlfriends' mothers over the years. I guess it's my way of having a mom. I have never understood the closeness my friends feel for their mothers.

As I stated in the beginning, I did not want to relive these memories or write this letter. I told my counselor, "Why do I want to write a letter to my dead mother?" She said, "Just do it."

In my six weeks in the program, I have learned one thing, which amazes me. I have learned that you did the best you could, and I have to accept that fact. I have the same disease as you, and my life hasn't turned out very well up to this point.

I do want to thank you for my life. Obviously, without you it wouldn't be possible. I hope God is looking over your soul.

Love,

Johnny

I stood sobbing before the group.

"Thank you, Johnny," a man said.

Another said thank you, and then another.

And then, as God is my witness, I felt the dark gray cloud lift from my shoulders, and since that moment, I haven't had a compulsion or desire to drink. The physical craving left me.

But as George Carlin once famously said, "I got the monkey off of my back, but the circus is still in town."

This statement couldn't have been more accurate. I had a lifetime of learning and change ahead of me.

CHAPTER 2
ADDICTION
TAKES ALL COMERS

ADDICTION DOESN'T CARE if you're rich or poor, young or old, male or female. It takes whoever it can get and is persistent, unrelenting, and unchanging in its ability to kill and destroy.

I became aware of this in the days and weeks after my letter to Mom.

I also learned that recovery is possible for some, but not for all. I could change, but Mom couldn't. Why?

The answer involves God, but it's more complicated than to say I am blessed.

When I saw my reflection in the mirror that first day in the rehab, I saw the bloated, jaundiced face of a body more dead than alive. It was a view into the abyss, and I was terrified by what I saw. And yet I still resisted change.

Addiction is a slow, lonely suicide. There is no doubt about that.

I've read that despair cannot exist in the presence of love. Though there were people who loved me, I can tell you there was little love in my heart. Instead, it was filled with despair and its brother, shame. This seems like a long fall for someone born into a family of wealth and all the opportunities that came with affluence. How could someone with every advantage reach such a point of unremitting despair?

The simple answer is that love cannot exist in the presence of despair. Love and despair can inversely crowd out the other, but for either to win out over the other, it must have an ally. The allies of love and recovery are God, the community, the fellowship of family, and programs like AA. The allies of despair are addiction, pain, trauma, and every other bit of provender that feeds self-hatred.

The deeper answer begins with my birth on December 17, 1958 in St. Louis, Missouri. There are only a handful of photos from that day, but the one that remains with me is of Mom, a couple hours after giving birth to me, her eyes tired, but a smile on her lips as she holds a vodka and tonic up to the camera. I'm sure there was a lit cigarette resting in an ashtray just out of the frame.

My sister and brother would join the party three and six years later.

From the outside looking in, everything appeared normal, but looking from the inside out, everything was a mess. Mom and Dad's marriage was for true love and was celebrated throughout the affluent and exclusive section of St. Louis into which my siblings and I were born. We attended the right schools and frequented the right country clubs. We associated with the right people. There was inherited wealth on Mom's side and a successful shoe business on Dad's side. There were private planes, a nanny, and a yard man.

What could possibly be wrong?

Years later, at the suggestion of a therapist, I asked Dad, "Why do I have so few memories of Mom?"

He didn't have to think for long nor did he ask the source or reason behind the question. "Lizzy and I put your mother to bed each night well before dinner because she was passed out drunk."

I suppose I could have come up with that answer on my own. I had a mother, but the woman who raised me, who was in every respect my mom, was our nanny, Lizzy. She was a tall and wiry woman who carried a tin of snuff in a pocket on her white uniform. Rarely did she not have a pinch of tobacco tucked in her lip, and one enduring memory is of her leaning out the kitchen door to both check on me and spit into the bushes.

She and I did everything together, and all my earliest memories include her. The fondest is of the two of us walking down the lane to our house each afternoon, my hand in hers. She welcomed me home from school, prepared all my meals—she fried everything— put me to bed, and made sure I said my prayers. As I fell asleep, she'd finish her work in the kitchen then come up to her room and listen to the radio as she sipped a Budweiser and spit into a tin can.

I knew she loved me because she told me so every day.

This was more than Mom ever said or did.

When I wasn't with Lizzy, I spent time with our yardman, Jasper. He had sad brown eyes, sagging skin, and graying hair at his temples that betrayed the toll of a hard life that was beyond my imagination at my young age. He was also kind and gentle toward me, and I was in awe of him. I've never known anyone stronger and remember watching him pull a tree out of the ground, roots and all. He let me help him rake the leaves down to a small creek to set fire to.

I was always with either Jasper and Lizzy, and the safety and security I felt as a child was due to their ever-watchful eyes and their presence in my life. I knew Dad loved me, but the demands of his business kept him away. Jasper and Lizzy were the constant sources of love and support that sustained me. They also set an example of hard work and honesty that I would later in life betray as an alcoholic, but the lessons proved stronger than the addiction.

Soon after I turned nine, Mom and Dad sat us three kids down on the couch in the living room, not far from the piano where our uncle played his annual drunken and perverse version of "The Little Drummer Boy." Dad began with, "We have something to tell you . . ." and it went downhill from there.

No one close to us had died—only our parents' marriage—and with that, I felt my first deep, incurable sense of insecurity. Divorce was uncommon in our social circle, and it was looked down upon, so all I knew of divorce was that it was bad. Life was going to change, but how much, I had no idea.

Dad finished with "Well, that's about it."

Then Mom spoke up. "Pack your bags. We're going to Florida."

Hours later, she awoke from a drunken stupor to ask, "Where the heck are we?"

My brother was three and Lisa six, and both sat across the aisle from Mom and me. At the sound of her voice, both looked at her and then me, wide-eyed and scared. Before we left Dad at home, he had come to me and placed his hands on my shoulders and looked directly into my eyes. "You have to be the man of the house now. Do your best in Florida."

"Mom," I said, "we're in Florida."

"Why?"

"Because the plane took us here."

A couple of men from the airport came onto the plane to help Mom, and they all but carried her to the baggage claim area. They waited with us as I watched for our bags, and then they helped her load our bags in the trunk and climb into a cab.

At the hotel, she said, "You know what to do" to me, and I signed us in and handed the clerk her credit card. The porters who helped Mom in from the cab held her up until we reached our room, and she fell onto the bed unconscious. I didn't know to fish through her purse or pockets for cash to tip them.

I suppose you could say this is where my memories of Mom begin. I was now part of the process of putting her to bed after she'd become too intoxicated to sustain herself. I knew she was difficult, but now I was finding out what that meant.

As our Florida trip played out, our entire family was worried to death about us in Florida. No one knew how we would get home if we managed to survive a week or two in our mother's care. As expected, things in Florida spiraled out of control until Mom was so neglectful of our care that the hotel called Dad. He sent a plane, and somehow we managed to get on it and fly home.

Dad knew this couldn't be sustained. Even in St. Louis with Lizzy and Jasper, there was no way to keep us entirely safe. So he called Mom's parents and brother and said, "We have to commit her to treatment. I'll take responsibility for rearing the kids until such a time as she's capable."

They agreed.

Alcoholics Anonymous wasn't recognized as a treatment program for women in the mid-1960s, so she was sent to the Mayo Clinic in Baltimore. She went through electroshock therapy, talk sessions, and everything else under the sun to try to get her to stop drinking. It worked for a bit, and she was released to live in an apartment in Baltimore. Over the course of five years, I saw her twice, and neither visit gave me the impression she was any better than before.

Meanwhile, life in St. Louis felt normal without Mom. There was Lizzy with her tin of snuff, spitting in the bushes, frying everything she cooked, and watching over my sister, brother, and me like a good and loving mother. Jasper and I worked in the garden, raked the yard, and I learned not to just the value of hard work, but also how to work hard.

Then, shortly after I turned fourteen, Mom returned with a new husband named Dale. He was a Navy man, a drunk, and temperamentally about as far away from what we were used to as possible. They moved into a large Tudor house only about two miles from us, and we could all feel the pressure in the air change.

She did not come back to earn our trust or find a way into our lives and regain our love. With her money and Donnie, the mafia lawyer, Mom was a blunt instrument intent on taking what she wanted. In this case, it was my sister, brother, and me from our father.

At about this same time, Dad married Celeste, a woman with a son and daughter and her own ideas of how our house should be run. The first changes were letting Lizzy and Jasper go. All that I'd known and all that gave security and consistency to my life were taken away. The God-sized hole that I seemed to have been born with was torn wider, and I started spinning out of control. Eventually, this would play a role in why I started drinking and why it worked so well for me. Being drunk equaled no pain.

After months of custody hearings, during which all three kids were deposed, the judge in his Solomonic wisdom granted custody of my brother, eight, and sister, eleven, to Mom. I was fourteen and so able to choose where I wanted to live. Dad. No question about it—Dad.

It did not take long for me to regret choosing Dad. It wasn't that I couldn't be happy with him, but as the older brother, I had failed my sister and brother. When they needed me most, I had let them go on their own into a den of drunks. The result was predictable.

After a year of abuse mixed with neglect, my sister managed to escape into a boarding school. This left my little brother alone. He suffered verbal and emotional abuse that evolved into persistent physical abuse. As if this wasn't enough, his emotional well-being was daily assaulted by the spectacle of Dale and Mom's marriage and life. Dale disappeared into bars and clubs in the morning and returned home in the evening, drunk and volatile. Mom drank alone until she passed out, often with a cigarette burning between her fingers. She wet herself often, fell and knocked her head or other body parts on table corners, and so on. She was unstable all the time. The only reprieve for my brother was school and Mom's drift from raving drunk to benumbed and then into unconsciousness.

I imagine that as my brother—still a little kid—fixed his own dinner each night with Mom passed out on the couch, he felt a sense of relief to not have Dale at home or Mom carrying on around him.

On the weekends I came to stay, I helped my brother with preparing food and anything else he needed. And then I'd escape the house for the night to be with friends and begin my own affair with alcohol. I remember sneaking out past my unconscious mom and waving goodbye to my brother as he, somber-eyed, watched me leave him alone yet again.

So I regret not doing more, not being there for my sister and brother, but I also have to ask, *Where was the cavalry?*

When Mom returned from Baltimore and her supposed rehabilitation, our lives changed overnight. This was especially true for my sister and brother who went from safety, security, proper meals prepared for them at proper times, and love to an asylum of active drunks. But Mom's behavior was nothing new.

Before alcohol fully took her over, Mom was a popular socialite, spending the day on the phone (and drinking) talking to her many friends. She was loved by aunts and uncles and cousins and was an established member of an elite community composed of many people who saw her descent into total alcoholism. These people did nothing, even as Dad paid thousands and thousands of dollars fighting Mom and her hired gun in court.

Dad did what he could, but he was one man against a level of drunken-selfish-wealth-crazy that was tireless in her determination to drink and destroy. Where was our community? Where was the cavalry?

"I am not going to be like my mother."

I remember the precise spot I was standing when I said that. It was early evening. Dale was still out drinking. I could smell the acrid odor of urine. The floor and couch around Mom were dotted with cigarette burns. Just behind her was the tabletop bar she used to pour her drinks. There were two empty bottles on the bar tray and one lying on the floor.

This was the millionth time I'd observed this scene. I was disgusted and filled with anger that she could do this to us, that she could let herself live this way.

And I hurt. What was so wrong with us that she could not love us enough to stop, to treat us and herself better?

My anger and feelings of betrayal and grief helped put me in a state that I describe as floating. If, during those years, anyone asked how I was in any meaningful way, I said, "I feel like I'm floating through life without any purpose."

Floating was a sort of catchall word that, to be honest, I didn't completely understand. I knew my life lacked direction. That was obvious. But I never knew what it really meant.

About two years ago, my brother turned fifty. He stood and gave a little impromptu speech to our friends and family. When I looked at my sister, she could not—or would not—take her eyes off him. She hung on every word, and in her eyes, I saw support and the nature of her love for him. It was unwavering, unconditional love born of a bond built through shared trauma. They grew up under Mom's roof, and all they had was each other, which is a closeness and affection for each other that has endured no matter the circumstances.

They went through something I am not part of because I chose to live with Dad.

At the same time, I was loved and taken care of at Dad's house, but with his new wife, I never felt comfortable or like I belonged to the family created by their marriage. I lived with one foot in each home, but neither felt like a home. Maybe these are the residual regrets and angst of a teenager, but I did not feel that I belonged to either home, or anywhere. So I went out looking.

Floating gave me the need to find people to call my own, and from that was born my ability to make friends and be a friend. My peers became my family as did the mother of the girl I dated through high school. And then one day, with a handful of friends, I had my first drink, and then another and another, and for the first time in my life, I felt like I found something that worked. For as long as I was in contact with this cure, my broken heart and soul didn't give me pain.

When you find something that works as well as alcohol, you stick with it.

I stuck with alcohol, even as my embarrassment and anger at Mom kept me from ever inviting any of my friends to her house. The only person that came close to meeting her was my high school girlfriend, but that fell apart when we arrived at Mom's house as she was being carted out on a gurney to an ambulance after falling and hitting her head. That was the only way she ever left that house, by ambulance with paramedics tending to some wound, and my brother and sister (if she was home) crying and scared.

I stuck with alcohol even as I left my brother alone in Mom's house, knowing what he would go through when Dale arrived home drunk and/or Mom came out of her stupor. I stuck with it through car crashes and encounters with the law. I held it even closer when my stepmother said, "You're going to turn out just like your mother."

I stuck with alcohol even as it pushed away the girl I loved and who loved me most in the world. She saw a future with me, but as my dedication to my new cure grew, that future faded away. Drinking crowded out anything positive that could have shown me a better way. My fealty to alcohol was total because I believed it gave far more than it took away.

Somehow, I managed to graduate from my prestigious prep school and was accepted to Drake University in Des Moines, Iowa.

"Wow" was all I could say on my first day of college. To my eyes, there were no rules, plenty of booze, and no apparent reason not to drink as well as an endless supply of drinking buddies. I had found nirvana and began a practice of daily drinking that lasted until January 5, 1999.

A year and a half later, Drake had enough of me and kicked me out. For the next year or so, I floated on alcoholic breezes that brought me to a private college in Columbia, Missouri. Just before graduating at the age of twenty-two, my brother called me to tell me that Mom had fallen, hit her head, and was in the hospital.

"Again?" I asked.

"Yeah, but this time's different."

"What do ya mean?"

"She's not going to come out of it. She's in a coma. I'd come home if I were you."

Maybe they had my brother call because they knew I couldn't say no to him.

I arrived at the hospital a day later. Tubes and wires ran from Mom to a catheter bag. There were IVs, monitors, and an intubation tube that ran to a ventilator. Her skin was sallow, and other than the slow rise and fall of her chest with the rhythm of the ventilator, there was no life.

With Dale and other members of Mom's family, we chose to take her off life support, and she passed away very quickly.

I would love to say that there were tears, but I had no feeling other than floating. I didn't know her other than seeing her passed out drunk on the couch. She had been an embarrassment to me and a source of torment for my brother and sister.

At Mom's funeral, there was only my sister and brother, great-aunt, Dale, Dad, and a minister. The socialite of her era was now dead, and her funeral looked like a scene from a pauper's life. This was the product of Mom's alcoholism, and I was headed in that direction, too.

###

After college, I moved to Austin thinking I could achieve some sort of geographical cure for what ailed me. Texas was good to me, and there were plenty of other drinkers to rub elbows with. In the midst of all the fun, I met a gal from Dallas, who I married, and I started a homebuilding business. The homebuilding business didn't work out, but I found my way into a hidden dog fence business and started what I thought was a good, normal life.

My wife didn't drink much, but that didn't slow me down. In short order, we had a daughter and then a son, both of whom I cherished, but neither was enough to put a dent in my drinking. My babies were no match for the progressive nature of alcoholism, which transitioned from a fun daily activity into a grinding daily need.

Seeking solace for the God-sized hole that was once again growing and gnawing at me, I sought a second geographic cure. I remember saying to my wife, "Let's move back home to St. Louis. That'll change everything for us. Fresh start. Whattaya say?"

So off we went.

CHAPTER 3
GOD VERSUS
THE DARKNESS

THOUGH EACH ADDICT travels his or her own path, the arc of the disease is progressive and consistent. At some point, the addict realizes they are in an ever-tightening cycle of use, and that breaking the cycle will require change.

What they fail to understand, or are unwilling to admit, is that it's the person who must change, not their surroundings or circumstances. Moving an alcoholic to a new town and career with a wife and young children does not change the alcoholic. It only changes the circumstances within which he will abuse alcohol and harm his family.

The reason for this is simple. Alcoholics lack a defense against the first drink.

When I moved my wife and children to St. Louis, I told my wife everything would work out. Through my family and friends, I believed, jobs and moneymaking opportunities would come like low-hanging fruit. Financial security would allow me to build a new life for my family, and with the hearty and virtuous pursuit of the good life, I could heal.

My wife—Texas born and bred—played the good soldier and came along for the ride. She knew the economy in Texas at that time was in a steep ebb. She also knew her husband drank too much and was in a steep ebb. I'm sure she hoped a new city, better prospects, and closeness to family and friends would placate my thirst for alcohol.

We had a house waiting for us, but nothing else. No plan. No job. All I had was a reliance on alcohol and a well-worn routine. I packed up my faults and bad habits in Austin and let them land with a thud in St. Louis.

Financial opportunities, rather than ripe fruit dangling from low branches, were slow to materialize. Family connections and well-connected friends never seemed to have a lead for me. Money became tight, and out of a sense of desperation, I started a line of accessories designed to match the high-end shoes Dad's company sold.

Meanwhile, my children were at that wonderful, beautiful stage of life where their mom and dad were the center of their universe and love flowed in equal measures to and from them. I was home each night to help with dinner and then play with them until bath time. With their soft hair smelling of baby shampoo, I lay with them in bed and read until I kissed each goodnight and left them to ease into their dreams.

I did all this with a beer or a drink in one hand. As they nodded off, I went out to meet friends at a bar or sat on our couch drinking until I passed out. These, I suppose, were the salad days. From the outside looking in, things seemed fine. We had a big house and beautiful children, I appeared to have good prospects, and our marriage looked like a happy one. There was family and plenty of friends, my daughter attended a good private school, and we were members of the same country club I'd been part of since I was a child holding onto Lizzy's skirts.

But it was a lonely life for my wife. Out of loyalty and the hope that we would find something better than what we had in Austin, she left everything and everyone she knew and loved back in Texas. In return, I left her home alone half the week to go drinking with friends or put a good buzz on at parties while she chased after and cared for the kids. The nights we spent at home, the couch and drinking were more important than maintaining a meaningful connection with her. I kept up the pretense of a close and loving marriage to family and most friends, but I was becoming more like my mother than not.

Even the club and private school had a pretension about them. I paid the club membership before anything else with whatever money I had for the month—bills and other necessities be damned— and my aunt paid the school tuition.

And my high-end line of fashion accessories? Mere grandiose thinking. I sold belts and other sundries made by one of Dad's manufacturers from a kiosk in a half-assed mall. Not quite the crowning achievement one would expect from my background.

Then things got a little better before they got much worse.

Running out of money and desperate for anything to call my own, I quit the kiosk and found, more like stumbled, my way into another hidden dog fence business. I was determined to make it work, which meant long days away from my family. The connection with my wife frayed and, on my own with a truck and tools of the trade, I discovered the pleasure of drinking in the late afternoons. By the time I came home, I had a six-pack under my belt.

I still helped with dinner if I was home early enough and helped the kids with their baths and read to them before bed, but I'd broken an invisible barrier that I could never again reseal. After putting the kids down to bed, I was back out at the bar drinking with friends. Back in Texas, I was home every night, but now I waved goodbye to my drinking buddies as they went home to their wives, and I closed the bars. If I didn't go out, my ass was on the couch with a fridge full of beer that would be gone by morning.

My drinking was tearing apart the fabric of my family.

One night, I stepped out on my family to go to a party where I bumped into a girl I knew from high school. We flirted and drank, but I returned home that night. A week later, I saw her in a bar, and we drank and flirted, and things progressed. She was attractive, but so were lots of women in our group. What drew me to her like a moth to flame was that she drank like I drank and was willing to drink in a hard and serious way.

She was my drinking buddy who kept at it long after our friends left the bar for their families. There was little emotional pull, and the sex held no meaning for me. It was about the addiction and the adolescent thrill at the danger of getting caught. Maturity stops with addiction, and I was still chasing the high and pleasure of an immature teenager without responsibility or cares. Instead of going home to my boring, middle-aged life, there was danger and risk and sneaking around and crazy nights of partying and drugs and bright lights and sex. I was a man seeking to live forever in a cocoon of alcohol and following each impulse as it came to me.

And yet, I was not without responsibility or people who loved me and depended on me to return that love. I felt their presence acutely, and that pushed me further into the depths of drunkenness. I can't say how many near heart attacks there were over the pain I would cause if my wife found out and the shame of exposing my true self to Dad, my sister and brother, and my extended family. There was a darkness closing in around me. My wife, children, and family mattered, and I cared deeply for them, but I would not and could not stop.

One night, after reading to my kids and giving my wife a peck on the cheek, I backed my car down the driveway and gave one last look at the bay window in the dining room that faced out onto the street. Within its frame, pressed against the cold glass, were the faces of my son and daughter. Their small hands waved goodbye to me. In a movie, I would have said enough, no more. I would have pulled the car into the garage and lain with my children until they drifted off to sleep and then begged my wife for forgiveness with tears streaming down my cheeks.

But this wasn't a movie. I gunned the engine, tears streaming down my cheeks, and I whispered, "How could I?"

The shame of that choice will never leave me.

It was obvious what I was up to. It wasn't long before the questions started. *What are you doing every night? Where do you go? Who are you with?* There were no answers. I'd reached a point where the lying and the stress of it exhausted me. I had lost my will to live a normal life and didn't give a damn. I would hurt everybody and anybody to get what I wanted and drink the way I wanted.

The end came when my wife's mother came to visit. My wife , if not me, was loyal to the institution of marriage. Her mother recognized the obvious and was loyal to her daughter. Her mother told me she knew what was going on and that I should just leave. My children and her daughter deserved better.

My wife pleaded for us to go to counseling. "Please, if you just try, I believe we can save this, save our family."

I agreed, but after the first session, it became clear I would have to give up alcohol to right what was wrong. I couldn't do it. In the car driving home from the appointment, I said, "I'm done. I'm gonna move out." And that was it.

One thing alcoholics try to do is normalize the role that alcohol plays in their lives. Mom did it by marrying Dale. He was a drunk, so he posed no threat to her drinking. What he offered was the patina of normalcy. Mom lived in a beautiful house with nice furniture—other than Mom's couch and drinking area—raised kids (sort of), and married a retired military officer.

I tried to do the same as Mom. I turned my alcoholic, adulterous lover into my girlfriend and set myself up in a divorced-dad apartment where I decorated the kids' room for their every-other-weekend visits. To square the circle, the next step was for the kids to meet the woman in my life. We went to a park and then dinner before I dropped the kids back with their mom.

It was a day or two later that the police called. "You've been accused of child sexual abuse. You need to come down to the station or we will come arrest you."

I can understand that my soon-to-be ex-wife would want to protect the kids from my drinking and a woman with little control of herself, but this was a lie. It was also an increasingly common lie used by divorce attorneys to gain the upper hand on an opposing spouse.

At the station, a cop explained the charges, to which I said this is crazy. He raised his eyebrows and shrugged as if to say, *What ya gonna do about it?* Then he told me I could not see my kids until I or the courts resolved the issue.

"How do I do that?" I asked.

"Hire a lawyer and fight the charges."

I went to my divorce attorney, but he said this was well above his pay grade and I needed a criminal defense lawyer. "Actually," he said, "you need the best criminal defense lawyer in St. Louis because this is serious stuff."

A moment later, and with a few drinks in me to steel my courage, I was on the phone with the lawyer my divorce attorney recommended. "You need to bring ten thousand dollars to me as soon as possible. This is as serious as murder."

"But I didn't do anything."

"Doesn't matter. In these cases, you are guilty until proven innocent."

I was in shock, and I was drunk—two states that would become my normal until January of 1999.

Ten thousand dollars was about all the money I had in the world, but with checkbook in hand, I went to see the attorney. He explained how these accusations work, that they were becoming common in high-conflict divorce cases, and then he laid out an initial strategy.

His secretary interrupted to say there was a society columnist from the local newspaper calling to ask about my case. My last name and connection to Mom's family—the cream of the society crop—meant this story was at least noteworthy.

"Look," I heard the society columnist say through the phone's loud earpiece, "his wife called and gave me a heads-up that Johnny's been charged with child sex abuse."

"Yeah."

"Well, I know this guy, and it doesn't seem right. I was hoping you could shed some light on this?"

"Okay, here's what I got. You're right, there's nothing to this other than a contentious divorce, and if you print anything about it, I'll sue you for libel."

And that was that.

To make a long story short, I asked to take a lie detector test. My lawyer asked if I was sure I wanted to do that, and I said, "Absolutely, I haven't done anything wrong."

The test lasted two hours and, in the end, the person administering the test said he was sure I didn't do it. That didn't stop my ex-wife or the prosecutor. My lawyer negotiated with the prosecution, and I agreed to admit to touching my daughter's shoulder. In exchange, the prosecutor required I have only supervised visits with my kids.

The deal satisfied the prosecutor but not my ex-wife. For the next three years, we fought it out in court as I battled for my rights to be a parent while my ex fought to deny me the ability to be a parent. It only ended after my ex accused me of abusing my son while we were in court in front of a judge.

The judge wiped his eyes with one hand then looked straight at my ex. "One more false accusation and *you* will lose custody of your kids."

After this, the battles subsided, but the fight and my own failings ruined my relationship with my kids. They'd been in the middle of too much conflict for too long. They'd had enough, and for their own sake, I had to let go, at least for the time being. As they became teenagers, they refused to see me or have anything to do with me.

Later, I realized it all was the consequence of my drinking. At the time, it all seemed so unfair, like I was the victim, but as with every hard emotion or personal failure, I had alcohol to take me away. As an alcoholic, truth and personal responsibility were attributes of other people.

If divorce, child sex abuse allegations, litigation, and lawyers were the only things that happened over this period of my life, who knows how my story would have turned out. But they weren't.

Police were a constant presence in my life. There were fights with my girlfriend. She'd try and scratch my eyes out, hit me, and that sort of thing, but what drew the calls to police in our quiet neighborhood was the yelling, slamming doors, and irrational behavior. You know, things I would characterize as annoying neighbor issues—my girlfriend and I being the annoying neighbors.

There were also three DWIs. I earned the first of these the night I met my girlfriend. I'd gone to a friend's father's funeral and then a bar after, which is where I ran into her. Some people say we all have baggage and that dating is about unpacking that baggage for the other to see. For us, we had to be sure our drinking matched, which it did, like a perverse cupid's arrow. The friends left the bar. She and I stayed until they bounced us out. I drove home alone, but I was so drunk that I drove down some railroad tracks. A cop saw me bouncing along and pulled me over at a crossing. A lawyer got me off with a slap on the wrist and no conviction for DWI.

The second DWI was more of the garden variety drunk driving. I swerved, and a cop pulled me over. Same lawyer, but this time the judge found me guilty of DWI and said one more and he'd throw me in jail. But he didn't take my license.

The third came in August of 1998 after a golf tournament at my country club. I ended up in the clubhouse with some of the fellas drinking planter's punch like it was Hawaiian Punch. The bowl dried up, the guys left for home and their families, and I rolled into my beat-up red pickup truck wearing golf shoes, a pink shirt, and white pants. A few minutes later, I swerved across the center lane and nearly hit a cop going the other way head-on.

He leaned down to see through the window, noticed my outfit and the empty beer cans piled in the passenger side, and started laughing. "Do you know you almost hit me?"

"Why, no, I didn't."

"Uh-huh."

I blew into a breathalyzer, which registered a point-two-eight alcohol level. That much alcohol in my body should have caused a blackout, but I remember everything. I remember the cop pulling me from the truck and leaning against the hood of the cop car as he searched me while another searched my truck. I remember the feel of the hard metal cuffs as they circled my wrists and the zigging click as he tightened them. I remember his hand holding my head down as I awkwardly stepped into the back of the cruiser with its blue lights spinning and lighting the surrounding woods and road. I remember the cars driving slowly by and the faces of the people staring at me. And I remember the booking, the taking of my fingerprints, and the metallic sound of the holding pen latch as they closed the door.

"Don't worry about the money," Donnie said. He was Mom's mob lawyer. "Remember, I got rich off all the work I did for your mom."

"Okay. Thanks."

"Three DWIs is not good. You know that, right?"

"Well, yes, but—"

"They could send you to prison."

"Just fix it. Please."

"I'll see what I can do, but you've got to stay clean and start going to AA meetings and find an outpatient program for alcoholics."

"Why?"

"Because you're more like your mom than not."

I went to an outpatient program for a few sessions but didn't want to have anything to do with AA. Somehow, through my supposed attempts at recovery, my lawyer convinced the judge to spare me any jail time. I lost my license for a year, paid a huge fine, and promised to continue with treatment—yeah, right. I kept drinking, and I kept driving, always terrified a cop would pull me over, and I'd go to jail.

Guys from private country clubs who wear pink shirts and white shorts don't do well in jail, or so people said, but I wasn't ready to quit.

As the divorce and subsequent legal issues continued, and I collected the DWIs, the people in my life faded away. It didn't happen all at once. They left in small groups as my behavior and that of my girlfriend became more unpredictable and harder to bear. On my own, I was only semi-stable, but with her, we'd get embarrassingly, pathetically drunk. Often, there were arguments that led to fights.

A few days before my sister hosted a small party, she called to say, "Johnny, I'm sorry, but I can't have you at this party. You're just so unpredictable that I can't have you."

Half of me was humiliated. The other half was relieved that I could spend the time drinking the way I wanted to. "I understand," I replied.

Another time, I flew to Cape Cod for a friend's wedding. I drank through the flight, on the way to the hotel, at the hotel, and at a party the night before the wedding. In a blackout, I pushed one of my best friends down a flight of stairs out of anger. Maybe he'd asked me to lighten up on the booze. The next day I started drinking early to take the edge off my hangover and shakiness. I made it through the ceremony but was too drunk and humiliated to stay for the reception. Later, a friend said I should keep my distance. They were done with me.

I knew I had a problem, and I knew I had the solution. I started drinking earlier and earlier in the day, which made it harder to maintain my business. I was so drunk one day that a client called me a cab to drive me home. Shame reddened my face as the cab pulled away from her home—a woman I'd known for years—but rather than take the lesson God was giving me, I started drinking more. Before long, I started waking up at about five in the morning to power down a few beers to make me feel better and stop the shakes.

I knew this wasn't normal, but addiction had now invaded every aspect of my life. I pushed away any thoughts that my drinking was destroying my life with another beer. The loss of friends and financial hardships—not making mortgage payments on the house I had moved into a few years after the divorce, missing truck payments, and on and on—I pushed away with alcohol. The DWIs, constant shame, constant fear, physical deterioration, mental deterioration, and the attempts by my dad and others who still cared to save me, I pushed away with alcohol.

What I didn't know then was that in each of these things—the inner chaos, outer chaos, and attempts by some to show their love—was God trying to reach through the darkness, to touch me and let me know He was there. Some of that light did get through, but alcohol quickly dimmed it.

As Christmas of 1998 approached, the darkness of total alcoholism had cast away nearly all God's light. He was not done fighting for me, but I was all but finished. My fortieth birthday was December 17, and I knew there was no one to share it with. I was alone. Even my girlfriend had left. I cooked a rack of lamb and made sure there was a case of beer in the fridge and a large bottle of wine. This was the last meal I ate until January 5, 1999.

This wasn't a conscious decision to starve and drink myself to death. Nothing I did in those days and weeks was conscious or intentional. It was all at the behest of alcoholism, which, like some sort of malevolent microbe, had taken over my mind, body, and spirit. Without anyone in my life or any responsibility, I was free, finally free of any restraints on my drinking. There was no plan other than to drink. I only rose to drink more or crawl out to get more booze. I was Gollum from *Lord of the Rings* in possession of the one ring to rule them all.

There was no space to fall further, other than death.

I drank for two hours then slept. When I woke, I drank again until I passed out. At one point, I woke in a panic that I had to go to a service call for a client at nine in the morning. I crawled into my truck and started the engine. As I backed down the driveway, I realized there was no light. It was nine at night. I kept driving for more booze and then back home to continue the slow suicide of end-stage alcoholism.

A knock on the door woke me.

"Who is it?" I asked.

"Dad!"

The warmth of panic wound up my spine at the threat of losing my freedom, the threat of a bit of light making its way in. "What?"

"You asked me to come over this morning to talk about your situation."

"When?"

"Last night when you called."

"I'm good. Thanks for coming."

I heard the scrape of the door as it opened, and I rose to my feet. I turned, and there was Dad—tall, well-dressed, and well-trimmed red hair. His eyes dimmed when he saw me, and his lips pressed together.

I wobbled a little, and my hands shook. "What do you want?" I knew what he was there to do.

"I'm here to try and help you."

"Shove off, Dad, I don't need it."

He'd dealt with Mom for years and knew what he was up against.

"I made an appointment at Exodus"—a treatment facility founded by a friend of his where—"they're expecting a visit from you."

I would accept treatment from Exodus, but not this time. "Good. See ya!"

He turned and left. The sound of the door shutting and his car pulling away freed me once again to drink unimpeded. Around nine in the morning, drunk and irritated, I couldn't get Dad out of my head and knew if I didn't go to that appointment, it would just eat at me. I drank a few more beers then pulled a coat on to walk to Exodus.

It wasn't far, and I started babbling at the receptionist. She had me sit, and a counselor appeared to take me into an office.

"Why are you here?"

I babbled at him for a bit—later, this same counselor would say I came in speaking Chinese—then I said, "My father wanted me to come, so here I am, and goodbye!" The shaking and thirst for alcohol was more than I could take. On my walk home, I stopped at a package store for more beer and drank at home until I passed out.

I woke to the phone ringing. "Hello?"

"See you in fifteen minutes," the woman's voice said.

"For what?"

"You called to ask if I'd pick you up for the Christmas party. You said you didn't want to drive."

"Who is this?"

She paused. "Beth, Johnny, it's Beth."

"Sorry."

"I'll be there soon."

I had no recollection of calling her. I was in a total blackout.

She was a friend of my sister's, and there would be a Christmas service and party afterward. I vaguely remember attending the service very drunk. I can't imagine what my family and their friends—once my friends, too—thought. I was a skeleton of my former self—my eyes and skin were jaundiced, I shook, and if you got too close, I smelled like a rancid beer. I have no idea how I got home or what happened other than a brief memory of the service. But I did make it home to crawl back into the darkness.

I now believed that I'd finally removed everyone and everything, including God, from my life, thereby freeing me to drink. I didn't even bother with foxhole prayers because I thought no one was listening. I was spiritually, emotionally, and physically dead. There was no more room left. No more chance of light entering and disturbing the darkness. I did not plan or commit to drinking to death. It was just what was happening.

###

If not for that phone . . .

I'd drunk dialed again, and when a voice came on the other end, I laid in, "Where is she?"

Whether I realized it or not, I was dying and wanted to take one last swipe at the girlfriend.

"She's not here," her mother answered.

In the Leonard Cohen song "Anthem," he sings, *There is a crack, a crack in everything; that's how the light gets in.* In an interview, he said, "This is where the resurrection is. It's in the brokenness of things."

The biggest of the cracks in my everything was that of a mother who could never be the mom I needed her to be. Like every child, I needed love and care, and it had to come from a mother. Though she lived into my third decade of life, she never lived for me. It wasn't the loss of death, but an ambiguous loss that I never mourned, that created a hole, that left as its scar a crack within my everything. It almost killed me, but as Cohen sings, this is how the light got in.

It came in that soft voice of a woman who suffered the ambiguous loss of her daughter. I can't know for sure, but maybe she saw something within me that she strained to find in her own flesh and blood—a bit of light, of hope. That was enough to enable her love and empathy, the instincts of a true mother.

"Can I ask you something, Johnny?"

God was speaking through the voice of a mother's love. "Yes."

"If I set up an appointment to check and see if you are an alcoholic, would you be willing to go?"

And I listened. "Yes, ma'am."

CHAPTER 4
LOVE AND THE
LIGHT IT SHEDS

WHEN I SAID YES to my ex-girlfriend's mother, I had no idea what I'd said yes to. I was at the depth of despair, most of the time lying on my kitchen floor waiting for life to leave my body. Instead, I rose into a new kind of torment, one where the best friend I'd had for more than twenty-five years was fighting and scratching for me to let it back in.

It didn't take much light in the form of love to singe the disease. That tender, soft voice—the voice of God in this world—moved me from the kitchen floor and overwhelming despair to recovery. It wasn't a single, simple step, and it didn't come easy, but it was powerful enough to be the first step away from physical and spiritual death.

The journey through the inpatient program, my first and subsequent AA meetings, and then outpatient treatment were the light of God's love in this world. The more light I let in, despite torrents of pain, regret, and the overwhelming desire to drink, despair loosened its grip on me. And then, as I wrote and then read my letter to Mom, I was finally released from the bondage of addiction.

Apparently, forgiveness is an act of love powerful enough to obliterate despair.

The hopelessness that took twenty-five years to grow and fester and then dominate my life and view of love and God took a mere six months to reduce to a shadow of its former self. But this did not mean it was gone. Nor did it mean I could rest and believe such pain could not return. Recovery is never recovered. It is a steady and persistent practice of receiving and conveying love through even the simplest of gestures.

This is God's will, and it is that thing we seek each day. It is also the twelfth step of AA: Having a spiritual awakening as the result of these steps, we try to carry this message to alcoholics, and to practice these principles in all our affairs. In short, we should rise each day with the question, *How can I be of service?*

None of this came easy, nor does it come easy. It is a practice, and some days are better than others.

After the letter, I attended two to three AA meetings per day, three aftercare meetings per week, and worked with a sponsor to guide me through the twelve steps. With it, I came to see the truth in the endless hackneyed and cliché sayings of AA: One day at a time; AA is for those who want it, not those who need it; GOD stands for Good Orderly Direction; okay is okay; yesterday is history, tomorrow is a mystery, and all we have is today, which is a gift; and, of course, the serenity prayer. These and other mottos and reminders were the handrail I could lean on as I climbed the steps.

The first three steps came relatively easy: admitting I was powerless and defenseless against alcohol, believing that a power greater than myself could restore me to sanity, and that I would turn my will over to that power. Steps four and five are where the work truly began.

I made a searching, honest, and fearless moral inventory of myself. This was a list of my character defects and the patterns by which I lived my life that had caused so many problems. When I got off track, my sponsor called me on it and made me recognize I was trying to repeat past mistakes with the hope the outcome would be different—the definition of insanity.

Along the way, I started to see a therapist. In our first meeting, I told him my story from start to finish, that I was born into a party that spun out of control and how I'd hurt everyone close to me. Worst of all was the pain and damage I'd done to my children. His next patient had canceled, so he used the next hour to tear me down. He called me a liar, a cheater, an adulterer, an alcoholic, a terrible and hurtful father, a self-centered and egotistical boyfriend and husband. He berated me for causing people great pain to avoid telling them the truth and told me that most of my adult life was a story of causing others pain because I lacked the will to do what was right.

All true. When he finished, I was speechless and in tears. I went home, and for the first time in my life, I sat with a candle and meditated. The next week, we set to work fixing all that Mom, addiction, and my own choices had broken.

The fifth step was making direct amends to all those I'd harmed, which was too long of a list. There was Dad, then my brother and sister, followed by my ex-wife, kids, friends, and then extended family. Some looked at me like I was nuts or like I was spinning yet another lie. I would have to show them my sincerity. Telling them I was sorry and wanted to change wasn't enough.

The hardest was my ex-wife and kids. For all good reasons, they didn't believe it was true, and there were precious little opportunities to show them my sorrow and commitment to change. My children have never fully accepted my attempts to make amends for how I have hurt them.

Making amends also included business clients, the bank that held my mortgage and payments on my truck, and anyone else I owed money to. Against the advice of my accountant—"Why stir it up if they haven't noticed?"—I contacted the IRS and worked with them to identify what I owed and establish a payment plan. I wanted to live life honestly.

Sobriety, therapy, working the steps, and making amends meant I'd also created the space to authentically and honestly work. My business remained on life support, but it was moving in the right direction. With that, I was on firmer financial ground for the first time in many, many years.

Legal problems were still an issue. While I'm sure the justice system was happy to have me sober, it didn't change the fact that I'd lost my license. I had no choice but to drive to work and meetings. I promised God that this would be it, that I would get rides everywhere else, and for the most part, I kept that promise. Perhaps God watched over me. Despite a few close calls, I didn't get pulled over that year. I completed a MADD program and classes to earn back my driver's license. Then, at age forty-one, I had the dubious honor of asking Dad to take me for my driver's test. I passed on the first go.

In taking the steps and doing the work to improve my life, I recognized I had to change not only where I played, but also my playmates and everything about living my life. I politely said no to the old drinking buddies who wanted to come back to me and yes to many new friends at AA and others who for many years—and for some, since I was a kid—had stayed away from the mess I'd become. And I started to learn how to do things, normal things, without alcohol. From my teenage years, I'd never cooked or barbecued without being drunk, nor had I gotten on a plane or driven without drinking. Hanging out with friends occurred at bars or anywhere else I could drink. Golfing was drinking with sticks. But now, I was learning whether I truly liked any of these things, or whether it was just the booze.

But despite the worries, anxieties, and new challenges, I trusted the process, and life was getting better, much better. My body felt light, and rather than ruminating on a catalogue of fears and worries, my mind and spirit were free to dream, hope, plan, and seek ways to be of service. I welcomed newcomers to the AA meetings I attended and helped ease them into the process. One of them would one day become the love of my life. I did all I could to help my family and new friends and avoid the isolation of home for the warmth of people and doing things.

At one point, I physically felt as though I was floating over the ground. This lasted for days and then weeks, which made me concerned it wasn't normal and I was floating right into a brick wall and a hard fall. I called Barbara, my counselor at the outpatient program, and described what was happening.

She laughed. "There's nothing to worry about. You're on a pink cloud."

"A what?"

"Pink cloud."

"Oh."

"It's a thing, really. Think of it this way, you dodged death and pulled yourself back from the edge, and now you've set a new course for your life. The work isn't done, but this sense of elation, of euphoria, is the realization and celebration that you are no longer on a path of dying, but one of living."

When I looked this up, I read, "These feelings are usually the result of an alcoholic or addict coming to the realization that they have avoided disaster and have set a course for a new way of life. This knowing is coupled with the realization there is a higher order to life."

In other words, it's a bit of a mystical experience. One of the things many alcoholics in recovery say is that they know there is a God because they changed when they could not do it on their own. A theologian would say it is a signal of transcendence.

And so the receipt and expression of love is an ineffable and transcendent light that has the power to send despair into the shadows and change one's life.

The subject of God, faith, spirituality, and religion has never been a comfortable one for me, but in recovery, they are subjects one must wrestle with. It is not a matter of belief in a specific faith or taking on a specific practice of worship. Rather, it's that you engage in a daily practice of identifying what your higher power intends for you as you move through each day and your life. The core and guiding principle is to seek ways to be of service.

Inherent in this, though, is the exploration of any past or current religious identity. Is a person in recovery meant to take up the Presbyterian, Methodist, Catholic, or Quaker practices and attendance that they left as the disease took hold? Or is it something else?

I still contemplate this question, but early in my recovery, I asked a friend, "Do you believe in God?"

"Sure!" he replied. "I tried for a good portion of my life to get sober on my own, and I failed. When I was finally in enough pain, I got down on my hands and knees and humbly asked God to help me. Right then and there, God lifted the compulsion and desire of addiction."

I'd heard some version of this story many times. It's a common experience among alcoholics, but what is less common is to then take up a specific faith because of that spiritual awakening. Some do, and some do not.

In my case, God removed my pain when I finally learned to forgive and release my resentments toward my mother. It was a spiritual experience and one that led to the mystical experience of the pink cloud and a deep belief in God. And yet I was not drawn back to the church of my parents. I'd seen too many atheists and sinners created within the pews of a church as just about anywhere else.

As my ruminations continued, I came to see faith, religion, and spirituality as related yet separate things. Religion is manmade, but faith and spirituality are God-given. I believe there is a God, and that belief includes the faith that everything in the universe is directly connected. Even the blade of grass you step on, the stone you toss into the water, or a person you injure exist in a sea of spiritual connections that encompasses the divine. Practicing that faith requires me to have compassion and forgiveness for others and myself and to be of service wherever I can.

This is not inconsistent with the goals of organized religions, but in my humble practice of faith, I feel a more immediate connection to the creator of all things. There is no intermediary or interpreter of God's will in my life, and I have found many varied opportunities to commune with God. And in all things, I have my eyes open for those transcendent indications of His will. And God is very, very good at letting me know when I stray.

Coming to this realization then freed me to begin my spiritual quest in life.

In AA, I found a new family. Not one that replaced my dad, sister, brother, and so on, but one where the connection was the desire to remain in recovery rather than that of blood. The people I met were a group who was just as screwed up as I was and were just trying to get better and stop the pain. We were and are the residents of Misfit Island from the Christmas movie *Rudolph the Red-Nosed Reindeer*. Individually, we were a mess, but together we were creative, strong, intelligent, and as tight as any group of people on earth.

We gave and received from being among each other, which meant that, when presented with a chance to be with these people, the operative word was *yes*. The first thing I said yes to was playing dominoes at Debbie's house. My instincts wanted to say no, too many people, I don't know how to play, and on and on, but I said yes.

As I have said, I hadn't done anything social without drinking in twenty-five years. The thought of sober socializing terrified me. But you know what? I had an okay time. Not great, not terrible, just okay. This was a huge accomplishment. I'd gone into foreign territory without my best friend, alcohol, and I survived.

This was the beginning of learning to say yes. It was also how I learned that even something as simple as bowling or dominoes was an opportunity to share and be of service in small informal ways. And in these moments was God, the light that helped keep despair at bay.

Saying yes to nearly everything also helped my social life start to soar. And the result? I learned how to live life sober rather than merely exist without alcohol.

Within my new family was one guy I became particularly close to. His name is Pete, and I met him at my first AA meeting.

"You know what?" he'd said as I stood holding a Styrofoam cup of coffee, every instinct telling me to run out of the room to a bar.

He looked to be about my age. His neck was thick and muscular, and his hair was black and cut short. He wore jeans and a brown sweatshirt with *NCAA Wrestling* written across it. He carried his body like a wrestler—strong, tensed, and almost squat as if waiting for an opponent to lunge at his legs.

"I took one look," he continued, "at your sad, bright red face and one-size-too-small Brooks Brothers suit and thought, 'There's a guy I can help.' You look terrible."

"I feel terrible."

"I'm Pete."

"I'm Johnny."

"Look, Johnny, we're about to start, but here's my number. Call me. I'm nothing special, just another guy white-knuckling it through each day and holding on for dear life."

I called him, and we hung onto each other for dear life. Over the first few weeks and months of my sobriety, we met up every night at an all-night coffee shop until it closed at 3 a.m. He told me he'd tried to get sober for twelve years, but it wasn't until he robbed a McDonald's in a blackout and a judge sent him to prison that he was finally ready to stop fighting. Lucky for us both, a parole board released him early, and he found his way to the same early morning meeting as me.

We went to silly AA dances where the men were on one side of the room and the women on the other. High school all over again except without the lubricant of alcohol. He knew many people, and I started to meet more and more of the same people each day. Slowly, we became part of normal society.

I liked this new me and this new feeling. Just as with alcohol, I became addicted to sobriety.

One of the terribly cliché yet true sayings of AA is *Anything that comes between me and my God is my new God*. Within this is a bit of hope and a word of warning. We are people who find new compulsions on a regular basis, and we must be aware of this. The flip side is that what we do in pursuit of God's will leads us in new and exciting directions.

Saying yes to life and this truth about God meant I was willing to try anything to keep the pink cloud going. I guess the pink cloud was my new god. I went to new and different AA meetings and different churches. I learned a variety of breathing exercises, studied meditation and yoga, and attended spiritual readings. I also started to enjoy new hobbies such as needlepointing, guitar, art, and so on, not worrying if I failed or not.

I was doing things for myself while helping others in the program. Then, when I was about six months sober, bigger life-changing opportunities came my way.

"Hey, Johnny," John, an AA friend, asked one day, "you wanna do a sweat lodge?"

"A what?"

"Sweat lodge."

"A lodge where we sweat?"

"Yeah, sort of. It's a Native American healing ritual led by a medicine man from the Pine Ridge Indian Reservation in South Dakota."

I thought for a moment and then said, "All in!" I had no idea what I was getting myself into.

To say that the sweat lodge was hot would be literally true but would miss the entire point. As John explained it, a sweat lodge is a sacred place to pray, meditate, learn, heal, and repurify ourselves bodily and spiritually. And the intent of each tradition that accompanies a sweat is to promote these ideals as well as the notion that we are to honor all religions, people, sexes, and ways of being. Before the sweat, I read, "We must always walk the red road in a way that honors others' views and teachings without sacrificing our own. All of these ways are good, none better or worse than the other."

These underlying ideas solidified and fulfilled my definition of spirituality, which is that we and everything are all connected, and there are many paths to God. Participating in this sweat lodge was yet another means to commune with God. The more I learned about the source of Native American sweat lodges and their meaning, the more I came to see them as an important expression of a sacred Native American legacy and an opportunity for the individual to seek a higher plane. As the piece I read before the sweat related, "With the introduction of alcohol and the inhumane treatment of native people, the need to repurify themselves and find their way back to traditional ways of living became evident. With the help of Medicine Men and Women, they could repair the damage done to their spirits, their minds, and their bodies. The sweat lodge is a healing place of spiritual refuge and mental and physical healing, a place to get answers and guidance by asking spiritual entities, totem helpers, the Creator, and Mother Earth for the needed wisdom and power."

Of course, the reference to the corrupting and addictive nature of alcohol, especially upon Native American populations, and the need for recovery struck a chord with me.

The day before the sweat, I refrained from caffeine, cigarettes, and sugar, and later in the day, I began a fast that would last through the sweat. On the day of the sweat, I arrived at the wickiup—a small lodge made of saplings lashed together to form a low dome and then covered with blankets—and nervously waited for whatever was to happen, well, to happen.

Not far from the lodge, a few men tended a fire within which were the river stones they would place in a small pit at the center of the lodge. The medicine man told us that the entrance faced east to signify that the rising sun is a source of renewal and wisdom. Before long, the medicine man walked among the participants—men and women—with a low-sloped clay bowl with smoking sage in it. He stopped at each person, allowing that person to wash the smoke over himself as the first step toward spiritual renewal.

We then crawled into the lodge through a small opening and moved around its edge in a clockwise direction until we were all sitting around the center pit. The medicine man then called for the attendants to place the heated stones in the pit in a manner that represented the four points of the compass. When they finished, the helpers closed a flap over the entrance, which left us in near darkness, the glow of the heated stones the only light. The medicine man then dipped a ladle into a bowl of river water and poured it over the stones. He did this a few times, and the lodge filled with hot steam.

Though every step of this ceremony conveyed the sacred and solemn nature of the moment, all I could think was, *Wow, it's really hot in here.* Though I never lost the sensation of being too hot, as the steam and heat rose, I fell into a meditative state. My mind wandered from thoughts held deeply within my own psyche to the prayers and observances of those who spoke when handed the talking stick. When it came to me, I shared without reservation my thankfulness to God and the new way of life I was in the process of discovering. And, as did others, I asked the Creator for forgiveness and forgiveness from those I'd hurt.

After about an hour, the medicine man signaled for the attendants to open the flap over the entrance, and we crawled out.

The air was cool, and we soaked in a nearby creek while more stones were prepared in a fire. A short time later, we entered the lodge again and repeated the process. In all, we did four doors—this is the term used by Native Americans, who also do things in fours. Each lasted about an hour.

It's hard to describe how well the sweat lodge worked for me. The mix of silent, meditative reflection and shared prayers, observances, and requests for forgiveness and guidance connected to that small, residual hole that I will always carry with me. It filled it with a sensation that I liken to a nirvana-like state. I was a changed person, and for the next few weeks I walked on air and felt a stronger connection to my spirituality and to the world creation.

I also learned that even while on a pink cloud, which Barbara said is a temporary state, life could get even better. I was only six months sober, but because I worked AA with honesty and a genuine desire for sobriety, turned my life over to God, and embraced saying yes to life, I was no longer engaged in a slow suicide. I was *living*.

A few days after the sweat lodge, a friend came up to me at an afternoon sober party for our Sunrisers' AA group.

"Howdy, Olivia."

"Hi, Johnny."

She was about fifteen years older than me with short blond hair, bright eyes, and a near constant smile. She was petite, and filled with abundant energy. She had committed her life to following the precepts of service to others, and God held in her Catholic faith. In her smiling eyes and gentle way, she was a force to be reckoned with.

She was about to change my life in a much different way than sober dominoes or a sweat lodge ever could.

"Johnny, what would you say to doing a REC with my group in a couple months?"

"Anything for you, Olivia."

CHAPTER 5
IF IT DIES,
IT PRODUCES MUCH FRUIT

FALL'S PAINTBRUSH WAS changing the once green canvas to one of gold, burgundy, tawny brown, and bright yellow. It was a cool, perfectly blue-sky day as I drove through the Missouri hills with the radio cranked so that each song rose above the wash of air blowing over me. Sobriety not only brought a sense of ease and calm to my life but also the ability to push for my business to succeed. The reward for that was the Chrysler Sebring I'd recently purchased.

Farmington is a mid-sized town with a downtown that's managed to maintain a sense of its rustic charm. The buildings that line its main street remind one of the way most of Missouri used to be—farm communities with a town center devoted to the needs of farming and providing a few idle distractions. Helping maintain this sensibility is that Farmington is the county seat, so it hosts the courthouse—a slightly ornate stone edifice—as well as an attractive red-brick town hall and a lovely little expanse of green called Long Park.

Keeping the community knitted together economically are the ubiquitous family farms, including a few wineries in and around

Farmington; the headquarters for Multi-Aero, a regional airline; SRG Global, a manufacturer of chrome-plated plastic automotive parts; U.S. Tool, one of the larger tool manufacturers in the country; Startek, a call center; BJC Parkland Health Center; Centene Corp., a health insurance-related company; USA Drug; and the Farmington Correctional Center, the place I would spend the next three days.

I was ebullient as I sped through the colorful countryside with the top down and the rock soundtrack to my late 1970s and early 1980s youth blared. The fact that I was about to enter prison, a place the thought of which caused me so much agony as I neared the depth of my addiction, was lost on me. I was fully ensconced in a pink-cloud moment.

As if back in high school, I wheeled into the parking lot of the motel the REC crew was to stay in and hopped out. All fifteen members of the crew seemed to have arrived at once and as a chorus said, "Hi, John."

I was all smiles—my face full of color from the ride and fresh air—as I pulled a suitcase from the back of the car.

"Looks like you're going on vacation," said Sandy, a middle-aged woman I'd met during the four prep meetings. These had been held every other Saturday leading up to today and were mandatory. Miss more than twenty-five percent of these meetings and you are off the team.

She smiled at me, and I smiled back then looked over at Olivia, the team leader and the woman who'd invited me to participate in this REC. I smiled, but she shook her head.

"What's wrong?" I asked.

"You are going to have to take this seriously, Johnny. I hope I didn't make a mistake including you in our REC."

"I promise, you didn't."

"We're not going into a country club, you know."

"Got it."

Each of us brought our share of the supplies we would need for the weekend and placed them in an organized pile in the motel parking lot. These included fresh fruit and vegetables, poster boards, bibles, hymnals, material for plays, musical instruments, costumes, paper and pens, and other odds and ends. All told, it looked as if we were going to entertain a camp of seventh and eighth graders, not a group of men imprisoned for everything from murder and rape to armed robbery and theft.

REC stands for Residents Encounter Christ and is intended to help a handful of select inmates, those men who have shown a desire to lead better lives, become more active Christians. The RECs are Catholic in their organization, but nondenominational in their practice. RECs are also more than opportunities to proselytize to a captive community. Yes, God's love is shared in ample amounts, but the emphasis is on personal and community growth. On the personal side, the belief is that the individual grows by changing attitudes to more successfully push back against and overcome internal and external challenges. And a community strengthens and grows when it works to develop its members (i.e., resist isolation and inward thinking) and by improving its environment (i.e., taking on the challenges of the community head-on).

In many ways, a REC parallels what I found and learned in AA, which is to live a life of service and one where I address my personal faults and failings head-on rather than through retreat and isolation. Helping to guide and support me as I work through learning these lessons is my higher power, God, to whom I turn over my life. Of course, it being AA, we have a great cliché: *Let go and let God.*

We transferred the pile of supplies into the two vans we would take to the prison and, surprisingly, there was still room for us. In a REC, there are two groups, the Outside Team (the volunteers) and the Inside Team (the prison's inmates whom we call residents). Each member of the Outside Team has a role to play: director, director-in-training, music minister, spiritual director, table leaders, table observers, and cooks and servers. The Inside Team has a few roles such as the inside coordinator who works with the director, cooks, and servers, and the rest are participants.

"Got everything?" Olivia barked.

So far, I was seeing a different side to Olivia than I had in the AA meetings we shared. I'd heard she was once head of a large corporate research department before she retired early. I could see that leadership quality coming forth, and there was little doubt why she'd been chosen to be a REC leader.

"Looks like it," came a hearty yet softer reply from Sister Mary Fran. She was a woman in constant motion with irrepressible, broad smiles. Just her standing with her hands on her hips, lower lip grinning and upper lip forming words was enough to return me to my driving-through-crisp-air-on-a-beautiful-fall-day mode.

I squeezed my body into one of the vans and looked out the window as we pulled out of the parking lot and onto the street. As we moved down the road, the chatter and titters of laughter subsided into a tense quiet.

"How far is it to the pen?" I asked.

"Correction facility!" Olivia barked back. "And it's six miles."

"Okay." I folded my hands in my lap and looked out the window. Any hint of the beautiful-fall-drive me was gone. My place in the pecking order was lower than low, obviously, and I should probably just keep my mouth closed.

We drove in silence.

The brick façade of the Farmington Correctional Center looks sort of like a 1950s-era high school. What put a lump in my throat were the guard towers, barbed wire, armed guards, and the noise that seemed to ventilate out through the brick into the air around us. There was an incessant sound of voices, steel, and anger. It was obvious I wasn't pulling into a country club parking lot. This was serious.

All my worst nightmares were contained behind the front door of this most unfriendly of places. If not for God, any one of my drunken turns behind the wheel could have landed me here as well as permanently altered the lives of some poor family. It was a sobering thought.

Olivia and Mary Fran went inside the entryway to meet with the warden and guards while I stood staring at the façade. My stomach was sour, and all I could think was *There but for the grace of God . . .*

"Johnny! Grab the fruit bags!" shouted one of the women in our team.

"Yes, ma'am." I felt reduced to my child-self, overwhelmed and wanting to do right but never managing it.

We piled the supplies on an apron of cement leading to the solid double prison doors. When Olivia and Mary Fran walked back through those doors, their mouths were set, and their eyes discontent.

"Pack it up," Olivia said.

"Why?" inquired everyone at once. I fought the urge to be relieved.

Mary Fran put her hands on her hips. "There was a fight in the prison yard, and everything is on lockdown. They don't know if the REC will be allowed this weekend or not."

"They can do that after everything we did?" I asked.

Olivia gave me a hard look. "They are one-hundred percent in charge, and we are at their mercy." She looked to the rest of the group. "Let's gather in a prayer circle and pray that the warden has the wisdom and compassion to allow this weekend's REC. Please pray for him and the residents of Farmington Correctional Center."

Joe, our religious and spiritual leader, began, "Lord, please allow this REC that is crucial to the serenity of the residents and outsiders to take place on this glorious weekend. We are ready and willing to serve you Lord in the capacity you see fit. We pray for those hurting and suffering. In the name of your son, Jesus Christ, Amen."

As a chorus, we responded, "Amen" and then packed everything up and went back to the motel.

Why aren't these people frustrated and angry? My teammates were smiling, laughing, and talking as if we were off to a park for a picnic on a wonderful fall day.

Even though my stomach was sick with anxiety just moments before, I was frustrated and angry that the warden could just say no. We'd put in a lot of work, and here we were. No. Can't do it. Go away.

In less than an hour, I'd gone from riding a pink cloud, to feeling like a misbehaving child, to having a panic attack, to being angry and frustrated. At the time, it all seemed normal, or at least it didn't cause me any moments of deeper reflection. Looking back on it now, it's obvious that, being newly sober, I had many character defects to work through. Even today, one of my biggest defects is patience.

This was not an issue for my teammates.

And, I also had control issues. I hadn't yet fully let go and let God, which means I didn't always comprehend that I am powerless over people, places, and things. I could hurt and help them and make appeals to get what I want, but I was not in control.

One of my counselors at Exodus, my outpatient recovery program, said, "Just say 'oh well' to everything and move on."

"Oh well," I whispered to myself. Now I just had to believe it. Then I said the serenity prayer. Yeah, I know, the most cliché thing about AA, but it works. *God, grant me the serenity to accept the things I cannot change, courage to change the things I can, and the wisdom to know the difference.* Cliché or not, it cuts to an eternal and important and all too forgettable truth: we are not in charge.

A cell phone rings, and Olivia says, "Hello? Yes, okay, great." She turned to her troops. "Let's go back!"

The queasiness in my stomach returned, but I also looked up into the sky and whispered, "Wow, you're good."

###

At about four in the afternoon—carts of our supplies in tow— we passed through the large double doors of the prison, heard their solid clank as they closed, and then were in a much different world from the one we left behind.

"One at a time and separate!" a guard shouted.

We came to a lobby area with cameras everywhere and guards watching us like hawks. I had thought we'd be treated like guests or coconspirators in the work of rehabilitating the residents of the prison, but no. The guards and prison valued what we were there to do, I think, but they also saw us as a risk. Which one of us was trying to bring in something illicit? Which was the joker who conned his way in here to help a friend? Who was going to cause a problem?

One at a time, we had a Polaroid picture taken that a guard placed in a plastic badge holder that we hung around our necks. The veteran REC volunteers also wore rainbow-colored necklaces with crosses dangling from them, which immediately got twisted up with their ID tag. In each photo, like with a mugshot, we were holding a sign that said VIC, which stands for volunteer in corrections. They treated us like the guests who didn't know it was time to leave.

Next, we passed through a gate, single file and with the guards' eyes fixed on us, into a waiting area and heard the gates clank closed and lock behind us. We were now in the prison. The guards looked uneasy, unhappy to have us there. I'm sure the fight that caused the lockdown was on their minds.

One guard stepped in front of us, his eyes wide with either fear or anger. "Eyes straight ahead," he barked. "Do not look at the prisoners in the yard. Do not get out of line. You are not allowed to speak to the prisoners."

Walking through the prison yard, we got some stares, a few catcalls to the ladies, but no interference. We made it across the yard then through locked steel gates into another building and then a large, open, sterile room.

During one of our prep meetings, Olivia said the prison yard quiets down on REC days. I also remember her saying the warden and guards hate, absolutely hate, REC weekends. It throws off the order of their carefully constructed world.

"When I say it's time to count, you will drop everything, remain seated at your tables, and do not communicate with the prisoners," said the same wide-eyed guard. "This is for your protection. If we ask anything of you, you need to do it immediately. We go everywhere in a group. Do not, and I repeat, do not separate. Do not get the phone numbers or addresses of the prisoners. Do not accept favors for favors. Do not promise anything. No unacceptable touching. If you need anything, ask one of the guards. We will do our best not to interfere with what you're doing, but I stress what we do is for your protection."

My nerves wanted me to break the tension with a joke, but if my lips moved even one scintilla, I knew Olivia and this guard would probably club me over the head.

The guard stepped back to the edge of the room and, with the other guards, eyed us as if we were perps.

"Alright, let's get things going," Olivia said.

We each had a role to play in setting the room up for the weekend and set to the work like busy, well-behaved bees setting up a new hive. There would be four outsiders and four residents acting as cooks in the small kitchen off one side of the room. They would also be our servers. There were seven tables, each of which held eight residents. At five of the tables, we would have table helpers/observers from the outside. The residents who would be cooks and servers — we called residents and outsiders on the kitchen crew *Wheaties* — had been through at least one previous REC and knew the routine.

This first day was called *Die Day*. As it is written in John 12:24, *Very truly I tell you, unless a kernel of wheat falls to the ground and dies, it remains only a single seed. But if it dies, it produces many seeds.* We were allowing the old self, the sinner self, the self that became an addict, made mistakes, and brought us to a place of suffering and sin, to die. From that metaphorical and spiritual death would rise a person with the capacity to not sin, to become something greater than what they were, to become someone who could reach for and fulfill their God-given potential.

As much as this day was given to seeking God's love and forgiveness and letting go of the life of a sinner, it was also about personal forgiveness and learning to love one's self again, or perhaps for the first time. It was a powerful message — one I am still learning and practicing — that, if embraced, could change the resident's lives now and forever. It was death as a symbol of hope.

As the REC is Catholic in its form, there are two important Catholic traditions held on *Die Day*. The first is the *Paschal Vigil Service*, which is usually held on Easter to observe and celebrate the resurrection of Christ. The second is the *Sacrament of Reconciliation*, which generally means confession and penance, though in a REC, we do not hold confession since many of the residents are not Catholic.

One of the most meaningful and emotional parts of this day is the writing of our sins on paper, which are then burned and the ashes placed on our foreheads. This symbolizes forgiveness by God, the father, of our sins. It is an acknowledgment that atonement is possible and with atonement a closer relationship with God. If we are genuine in our observations and practice of these rights, the hope and prayer for this day is that the residents, and even the outsiders, undergo a *Metanoia*. This means a transformative change of heart. It is a rebirth of our spiritual life and a recommitment.

As we worked to transform the room, a solemn and dark mood overcame my fellow outsiders. There were no residents at this point. Dark-themed posters and banners, some from past RECs and others created for this REC, were hung on the white walls. Our music guide, Tony, sat in a corner playing gospel music on his guitar. A few team members hummed quietly. We laid the day's supplies on the table: cups, pens, pencils, paper, stalks of wheat, name cards, Bibles, hymnals, and programs. In the kitchen area, Wheaties were busy preparing for *Die Day*. We had brought fruit, vegetables, crackers, cookies, juice, water, soda, and plastic utensils.

It was six in the evening, and we were racing to get things done so that this most important piece of the REC could happen. Still wanting to control things I could not, my anger at the warden's decision reared its ugly head as the people around me prepared as if all was normal. *We aren't going to have enough time to complete or create a sense of Metanoia. The whole weekend will be a waste,* I thought.

I hadn't yet grasped that okay is okay and that it's all right to do the best we can. I'd barely accepted God into my life, but I said the serenity prayer again, and then again, but slowly, hearing each word and holding onto the message of it. I was calmed by it and continued to perform my role in the setup.

"Everyone gather around," Olivia called out.

She was a natural leader and had the respect of everyone. I hadn't seen this quality in her in the rooms of Alcoholics Anonymous.

"In a few minutes, the residents will come through the doors, and I want quiet. This is a day of penance, atonement, and reconciliation. Remember, this is a somber day. No smiling, no jokes"—maybe I was feeling defensive, but it seemed she glanced at me—"and certainly no hugging. These residents are here to die today so that they can be raised tomorrow."

A chorus of "Praise Jesus" and "Lord help us to help ourselves" rose. People raised their hands to the ceiling, and I heard personal prayers. They were excited yet calm, where I was nervous and unsure. Being in a prison, a place I had feared for so long, was new to me, but so too was witnessing the unquestioning, undeniable, unconditional love and devotion these people had for God and His son Jesus Christ. It was moving and provided a measure of comfort and reassurance.

I am not in control here. God is. Let go and let God, I thought to myself.

Olivia raised her eyes. "Okay, Mary Fran, will you please lead us in prayer?"

"God, please give my fellow outsiders the strength to carry the message of your son Jesus Christ to these residents. Please let them be open to hearing your word so that they may pass it on. Please allow these outsiders to have the patience, compassion, and understanding to work with these residents to help them on their journey forward after this REC. Please allow the residents to accept this weekend for what it is and be open to the word of Your son, Jesus Christ. Let these residents hear your message, take it in, pass it on to their fellow residents, and take it to the outside when possible. In Jesus's name, we pray. Amen."

What in the world had I gotten myself into? I was nervous, afraid, happy, sad, moved. It had been just a few months since I was lying on my floor waiting to leave this earth, and now here I was, sober and in the place I most feared.

"Please line up on each side of the door to form two columns leading into the room," Olivia said.

We did this—eight outsiders on either side—and each person tilted their head forward and prayed quietly. I was the only one looking around and not saying a prayer. My stomach began to hurt, and there was a lump in my throat. The fear of the unknown is a big one, and I had it going on right now. I said to myself, *These others made it through their first time. I can as well.* I put my head down and said the serenity prayer, the only prayer I knew from heart. It worked, and I felt calmer and ready for what was to come. A smile passed over my lips.

Bang!

"Get back in line! No talking! No touching! You move when we say move! We say count, you line up! If one of you gets out of line, the entire weekend is over! Got it?"

Outside the door and down the hall, sixty men, their voices loud and clear, deep and strong, said as a chorus, "Yes, boss!"

The smile was gone. Serenity was gone. My heart was beating a mile a minute, and I felt ready to jump out of my skin. "God, grant me the serenity to accept . . ." I began, but the fear would not relent. I remember hearing in a movie not to let them see the fear in your face. Tough it out. That was not happening. I had fear written all over my face in big crimson letters.

Then came the sound of sixty inmates and ten very serious prison guards marching toward the door. The sound of their soft, rubber-soled shoes moved closer and closer. There was nowhere to run, nowhere to hide in an open room approximately forty-feet-by-forty-feet. No, I was fully in.

The door opened, and a guard passed through. He looked at the sixteen of us—we were mostly older, soft-looking folks who posed no threat whatsoever—and shook his head. "All right, file in!"

"Yes, boss!"

One by one, sixty men of every description wearing gray uniforms passed through the door, smiling. All sixty of them. At first, I was silent as the other outsiders gave each man a solemn greeting. My spell broke, and in a soft, tremulous voice I greeted them, too, into the sanctuary we created for them. As the last filed in, the guards took up positions around the room. They were omnipresent and fierce-looking, but they also seemed to be curious. About what, I didn't know. Perhaps they were wondering which of the prisoners was going to cause a big enough problem to shut the whole thing down. Or maybe they thought we were in over our heads.

Olivia stepped forward. "Welcome, residents. Please find a table, fill out a name card, and have a seat. There are seven tables, so eight of you at each table. Resident Wheaties, please go directly to the kitchen and help the outside Wheaties."

It was obvious that Olivia knew the residents who were serving as Wheaties. Each gave her a slight hug, nothing to cause the guards alarm, and went immediately to the makeshift kitchen.

Tony, the music director, began to play "Amazing Grace" on his guitar. It wasn't the hopeful, more upbeat version, but softer, slower, somewhat sweeter, and also more of a lament. A few residents sang the words in soft whispers. "Amazing grace, how sweet the sound, that saved a wretch like me . . ."

The moment was surreal, and I didn't know whether to cry, laugh, feel sad, or feel happy. A flood of emotions overpowered me in a way that felt like when I finished reading the letter to Mom. I was letting go of something, but also giving something. I couldn't place my finger on it, but there was a divine quality to it.

"Please take your seats. There are some announcements before we get started," Olivia said above the soft guitar and whispered singing. "First, welcome. We are happy you all are here and that you have the opportunity to participate in this weekend's REC, themed *Dying and Changing*. Please turn to page eighty-four of—"

"Count off!" yelled one of the guards.

The residents stood then walked to the back wall to form a line, their backs to the wall, and counted off, one through fifty-six. The men in the kitchen stood in a row and counted off one through four.

"Okay," said the guard. "A little faster next time."

My control issues kicked in. *What a jerk!* I thought. *We are barely starting, and they already need to prove their control over the residents.* I'm not sure if I was more scared of the guards or the residents.

The residents sat back down and looked at Olivia, who stood quietly in the center of the room. She looked so small and vulnerable as compared to most of the residents—I felt small and vulnerable compared to them—but when she spoke, there was calm and strength in her voice.

"As I was saying, please turn to page eighty-four of your hymnal and let's sing 'Amazing Grace,' shall we?"

Tony strummed the first few chords a bit louder than before and paused at the first stanza. We were awkward and disjointed at first, but the guitar gave us a steady rhythm to follow, and soon our voices aligned to the lyrics. My voice was soft at first, as were others, but the other outsiders, those who'd done this before, sang with strength and faith. I lifted my voice, "'Twas grace that taught my heart to fear, and grace my fears relieved. How precious did that grace appear, the hour I first believed . . ."

All seventy-six of us, including a few guards, sang in unison, and our voices gained in strength so that I felt as if I were in a gospel choir. The beauty and power of the song touched me, and within its melody, I saw and felt my own recent coming to grace.

A handful of guards left the room and chatted as they kept an eye on us from the hallway. It was said that if a resident got out of line, the other residents would immediately jump on him to stop whatever the issue was. They didn't want to lose the privilege of this weekend.

I was at table seven, and with the end of the song, we took a moment to introduce ourselves. It was obvious that the men were going to play their cards close to their chest. They said their names and immediately looked down and fidgeted with the items on the table in front of them. Some read from the Bible, others looked around for friends. Low mumbles floated like a layer of mist with the sounds of the kitchen crew rising above every so often.

Mary Fran, our spiritual guide, stood. "Let us start the weekend with the *Lord's Prayer*."

She began, "Our Father, who art in heaven . . ." The outsiders chimed right in at *Our Father*, and with the *who art*, the residents and I stumbled and mumbled into it until we reached *thy kingdom come* where we found our footing. In harmony, our modest and newfound congregation carried the prayer through *thy will be done, on earth as it is in heaven. Give us this day our daily bread, and forgive us our trespasses as we forgive those who trespass against us. Lead us not into temptation, but deliver us from evil.*

And then, as a chorus, *Amen!*

"Okay," Olivia said as she returned to the center of the room. "Let's start filling out on a piece of paper your five thoughts of Jesus Christ, and then we will discuss them among our tablemates. Quietly, please. Remember, this is Die Day."

The residents had prepared for the weekend, so they knew and understood the sequence of events and what it meant that it was Die Day.

Tony started quietly playing "All Hail the Power of Jesus Name." A few of the men at my table hummed or sang in a low whisper to the melody . . . *Let angels prostrate fall, bring forth the royal diadem, and crown him lord of all . . .*

I didn't know this song much less have a clue to the words, but I mumbled along with the residents.

"Hey, Joe," I said to a man seated next to me. "How do you know the words?"

He looked at me like I was an idiot. "We got nothing but time, man. We know the songs, and we know the bible verses."

I looked around, and what I hadn't noticed when the residents paraded in was that nearly every one of them carried a personal Bible. They looked worn, and little torn pieces of paper marked individual pages. These Bibles were used and loved, not like the pristine Bible I had grown up with or the Gideon Bibles you see in hotel rooms.

I felt as if I were an idiot and that I'd insulted these men within the first few minutes of the REC.

The Wheaties walked among the tables with trays of juice, carrots, and celery for each table.

"Praise Jesus!" went up a collective cry. "Amen, brother!"

These men had not seen juice and vegetables this fresh in a long time. Like piranhas, they stripped the food from the tray in sixty seconds. Then there were smiles and small talk. In the time it took for them to eat, something had changed. The mood lifted and became not quite lighthearted, but lighter.

Dorothy, our table leader, asked the men if they had their cards filled out. Then she went around the table asking each man to name one thing Jesus meant to them from their card.

"Love."

"Salvation."

"Forgiveness"

"Friendship."

"Warmth."

I had to wing it. I'd barely come to believe in God and was still learning what it meant to turn my life over to Him. I hadn't yet considered what Jesus meant to me or even to understand His divinity. I accepted God and faith, but there was conflict with religion. Church had created and hosted more sinners than I could count, but here I was seeing, feeling, witnessing the power of this Catholic-inspired weekend of faith.

I looked around the table. Each man looked at me and waited. "Compassion," I said. I took this directly from my definition of spirituality.

After the lists, a resident stood and gave a brief talk on Christian ideals and maturity and how to achieve them. I was moved by his fluency with discussing not just the Christian ideals, but also his own connection with and perception of his faith. This was not an off-the-cuff talk, but one that was prepared, intentional, and moving.

Then Mary Fran stood to give the *Paschal Mystery of Jesus*. This is a principal tenet if not *the* central tenet of the Catholic faith. It is the story of Jesus's blessed passion, death, resurrection, and then glorious ascension. But it is more than that. It is a symbol of the ability of humans to die as a means to release themselves of sin and then to rise again to go forth through life with the Lord and His son, our savior, Jesus Christ. The *Paschal Mystery* is also the source of one of the Catholic Church's most sacred sacraments, *The Eucharist*, which is the taking of the body and blood of Christ to be close to Him and remember Christ's sacrifice on the cross.

I was so caught up in the moment that I can't remember the specifics of what Mary Fran said, but since then I have carried the message of her words. Change, in many circumstances, requires a death of the will to fight redemption. Often, pain is a precursor and important component to bringing the individual to a point of exhaustion, to where they not only need to change but want to change. This was an obvious theme in my own life. I had to take my alcoholism to the edge and peek over into the abyss before I was willing and wanted to change. It took being near death to want to live.

Maybe I am not unique, I thought. These men seem to get the drift. They are convinced and believe that Jesus died for all our sins and will be resurrected. It's incredible how I almost—

"Count!" yelled a guard.

Unbelievable! We are almost done for the night, and they do this again.

The residents dropped everything and lined up against the wall. Fifty-four, fifty-five, fifty-six . . . Then they sat back down. Then a guard yelled, "Time to go! Line up!"

It had been four hours since the residents arrived, but it felt as if we'd only begun. We said goodbyes, and then they marched from the room, the smacking of their soft rubber-soled shoes subsiding as they paraded away.

"Very successful Die Day," Olivia exclaimed. "Let's pack up and head out."

"But Olivia," I protested, "we missed the talk of the *Prodigal Son*, the talk of the *Metanoia*, the talk of forgiveness and the service of the ashes, the sacrament of reconciliation, and the *Paschal Vigil Service*."

"It doesn't matter, Johnny. Let it go. We have a full day tomorrow, and that is what's important right now."

There was very little talk on our way back to the motel. Once we arrived, we said goodnight and went to our respective rooms. My mind was full of thoughts, and I had a difficult time sleeping. Our worlds were so far apart, yet so close together. If you look for the similarities and not the differences, you could almost imagine being these men.

The alarm went off at six-thirty the next morning. I took a quick shower and met everyone in the lobby for a coffee and Danish.

"What did you think, Johnny?" Olivia asked.

"I think it's going to take a while to process it all, but so far, so good."

"Wait until today," she said then walked to sit with Mary Fran.

CHAPTER 6
OPEN YOUR EYES,
GOD IS HERE

THE RESURRECTION OF CHRIST is powerful. It is the foundation of Catholicism and of the Christian faith. If, as the Bible posits in John 12:24— " . . . unless a kernel of wheat falls to the ground and dies, it remains only a single seed. But if it dies, it produces many seeds—Christ's resurrection produced many, many millions of seeds.

The second day of the REC is called *Rise Day* because it reflects this value of faith that it is not just transcending death, but the use of that reborn life that is what matters. Christ did not rise only to walk away and live out his days. That was not his calling. His calling was to a much greater purpose, and that is what we wanted to inculcate within the residents of our REC.

Growth comes from giving and sacrificing and being aware of and responding to the needs of others. Jesus is the example, and he walks with us. So if we see him as our brother and build a life based on His example, then we walk with Him. That's where goodness lies.

But there were no palm fronds, and there was no warm desert for us. Instead, on a cold, gray day in Missouri, we packed into two vans overloaded with our supplies and drove to a loud, colorless, and fearful place.

We went through the same procedure at the prison as before. The guards' demeanor had not changed one iota.

Once inside our little sanctuary, Olivia stood in the center of the room. "Okay, folks, it's Rise Day. Please put up the new posters and let's get the rest of it set up for our residents."

Within fifteen or twenty minutes, the room was transformed into a fun, party-like atmosphere. There were streamers, balloons, and colorful posters on the wall. As opposed to Die Day, this day was about rising to a new life within which we can be fruitful and see Jesus's presence in our lives. It would be a hard day, but also a good day.

I heard the cooks and servers in the back busily preparing the day's goodies. Olivia and Mary Fran were going over notes. Tony was playing upbeat gospel music. The rest of us continued to transform the room.

"Everybody, it's eight o'clock. Time to line up," Olivia said.

As we stood in line, murmuring to the person next to us, we heard the residents approaching. Then, in that echoing tin can of a room, burst forth, *Jeremiah was a bullfrog . . .* It was loud and sudden, and I turned to see its source, and there was Tony turning up the volume on his boombox.

He was a good friend of mine—

I smiled and looked to the others who smiled as well.

I never understood a word he said—

A woman clapped her hands against her hips.

But I helped him drink his wine—

Another woman swayed a bit.

He always had some mighty fine wine —

And then with a little urging from Olivia and Mary Fran, we all joined in.

Joy to the world, all the boys and girls now —

We started clapping, stomping our feet, and singing at the top of our lungs.

Joy to the fishes in the deep blue sea —

The door opened, and a guard looked in, frowning, but the residents entered smiling and laughing. We gave them high fives and patted them on the back.

Joy to you and me —

There were cookies, and we danced around the room to the rest of that song and two more. What a difference from Die Day. This, I liked!

"Okay, let's settle down and go to our tables," Olivia said. "Today is Rise Day, and from the scripture of John 12:24, *'If the seed dies, it produces much fruit.'*"

As if on cue, the Wheaties brought out assorted bagels with butter, cream cheese, and juice. The smiles of the residents were infectious, and we started in on the bagels while trying to sing "What a Friend We Have in Jesus."

> *. . . O, what peace we often forfeit, O what needless pain we bear, All because we do not carry everything to God in prayer —*

"Praise Jesus!" Who said that? It was me, experiencing that moment as we sang. Olivia gave me a wink, and a few of the outsiders and a few of the insiders smiled at me. It felt good and welcoming, and perhaps for the first time, I understood the word *Fellowship.*

We finished singing, and Olivia stepped to the center of the room. "Okay, let's start with the *Bible Enthronement.*"

Four people carried the Bible, two candles, and a crucifix to the altar and gently placed the items down as they had the day before.

"This is the word of God!" Mary Fran professed.

"Amen," we all responded.

I was elated and couldn't wait to start with the rest of the day. There was a resident, Sam, sitting next to me. Yesterday, his face was hard and impassive and betrayed little about him. I turned to him, and there was a wisp of a smile, and his eyes, rather than narrow and scanning, were a bit more open, less tense, taking things in. I looked around the room, and the residents were a bit lighter, a bit brighter, though I would not say transformed. Maybe for a moment, they'd forgotten that outside of this room a cell waited for them.

Dorothy, our table leader, asked us how the night was and how we felt about the REC. From their eyes, I could sort of tell there were mixed emotions. The food and drinks received unanimous approval, but having only four hours the night before didn't give the residents time to form an opinion. *Today we have a full day, I* thought, *and that will be a good measure of how things are going.*

With the table quiet, reticent, Dorothy said, "Okay, what does rising with the Lord mean for each of you?"

The question went around the table. In a voice that formed a question more than raised a statement, the first resident said, "I can rise up and have a new life."

The next man said, "I dunno."

The third, "My sins will be forgiven."

Sam said, "I don't have to worry about my past crimes"—he paused—"and maybe my wife will take me back."

Another man shook his head, and the next looked at Sam and said, "I'd love to think it means my children will come back into my life."

"I wanna add something," Sam interrupted. "I can go to school and find a decent job instead of walking the streets."

There was desire in him.

Dorothy took a turn. "I get to have opportunities like this one to reach out to others."

The man who only shook his head, a serious-looking man named James, looked at Dorothy. "What are you doing here anyway? My family, my friends don't come visit. Why are you here? Why are you spending three days here when you could be outside, the one place I want to be more than anything in this world, enjoying life?"

Dorothy took a deep breath. Her hands shook a little as she spoke. "I have come in the name of God and his son Jesus Christ to bring the good word to you. I have come to reach out and let you know that people do care and there is hope for salvation in this life and for a good life. I believe your sins can be forgiven, and you can have a fruitful and productive life. I am not here to judge you for I am a sinner as well."

"Amen, sister," a few men affirmed.

"You're no sinner like me," he responded.

I sat forward in my chair and looked at James. "To be honest, I'm here for myself. I *have* sinned, and I *am* trying to lead a new life to help others, and in the end, I help myself. Considering my sins, I could have just as easily been in here side by side with you.

"I've hurt many in my life, and for a long while, I only cared about myself. And I lost everything. My wife, my children, my friends, and nearly my life. I brought myself to the point of death chasing my sins, but for some reason beyond my knowing, God picked me up and saved my sorry soul.

"I don't deserve the life I have today. I truly do not.

"When Olivia suggested that I join her on this REC, and I agreed not knowing what I was getting into, I thought I was so different from you residents. But I'm not. Not at all. Luckier, perhaps, but we are identical, my brother. There is no reason that I didn't end up here or dead that I can think of other than God. Why me? I have no idea. It's truly a mystery."

I'm not sure where that came from. I doubt I'd been that honest up to that point even with my AA sponsor, but there was an immediate sense of relief. I looked from James to the other residents, and I thought maybe there was a little more acceptance. I had no idea what James thought.

"Okay," barked Tony. "Please turn your hymnals to page sixty-four and let's sing 'Turn Your Eyes Upon Jesus.'"

And so we started in with *"Turn your eyes upon Jesus, look full in his face ..."* as the Wheaties prepared trays of fruit, cookies, and soda. We finished the song, and to loud applause, the trays were set on the tables, and the piranhas took over.

I chuckled a little as I thought about how the food would disappear in my prep school cafeteria seconds after being served.

"What's so funny?" Sam asked.

"I was just thinking about when I was in prep school and the food arrived. You all reminded me of that."

His smile withered. "What's a prep school?"

I shifted a little in my seat. "It's a high school where they prepare you to go to college."

"A what?"

"A preparatory school."

"Never heard of anything like that."

Though there were great similarities, there were also great differences. I had all the advantages the world could offer. I imagine many of the residents didn't have access to most of it. I decided the last thing I wanted was to offend anyone. Best to tiptoe around this and similar issues.

I looked at Sam. "When my alcoholic mother and my father divorced, they sent me to this school."

"To get you out of their hair?"

"Yeah, pretty much."

"Got it. My father was long gone, and my mother worked two jobs. I kind of became a street kid and got into all sorts of trouble and ended up in a gang. Eventually the cops busted me, and here I am.

"My mom did the best she could, so when I get out of here, I want to straighten out and help her."

"Sounds good to me, Sam. I'd love to help my mom out, but she died of alcoholism."

"Sorry, man."

"Thanks, Sam, but it was her choice."

Mary Fran stood and shouted, "Christ has risen! Need not be afraid. Do not remain entombed in your sin. Rise up, like Jesus did. He is our light and guide. Follow His example. Please, Tony, let's sing 'Hallelujah.'"

I expected something akin to the Mormon Tabernacle Choir singing Handel, but Tony cranked up Leonard Cohen's "Hallelujah" on his boom box.

Now I've heard there was a secret chord, that David played, and it pleased the Lord . . .

We all sang along, some haltingly as we struggled for the next lyric, but it was a beautiful song that created a moment, an experience of fellowship.

With the last, soft hallelujah rose a loud, joyful, "Praise Jesus! Yes indeed! He has risen!"

With that, Tony played more music, and we danced and sang and in one moment formed a human train that danced around the room. The guards were getting irritated and concerned and watched closely as some of the residents had their hands on the hips of female outsiders in front of them. But there were no problems. Just a moment of escape for men imprisoned for years.

"Whew!" Olivia exhaled. "Okay, back to the tables. I want you to discuss at your tables what it means to be part of a community that shares the same beliefs. We are God's chosen people."

A chorus of *amen* echoed through the room. It was spontaneous and came not from every voice, but from everywhere. There were those who remained enigmatic and reserved, as if they felt a need to protect themselves. But even in the eyes of those who remained quiet, it was a different mood than from the day before.

And then, a man at my table named Michael spoke for the first time that weekend. "My community is this table. I feel like I have come down to breakfast with my brothers and sisters." He smiled and looked down to his hands that were folded in front of him then looked up. "Yes, this is a good day."

James edged forward. "Word, my brother."

Dorothy looked from James and Michael to the other men and asked, "What do you think community means?"

As the others reflected, Sam spoke up. "You know, we have our own community in here. Many of us have brothers, cousins, and relatives in with us."

"My daddy is in here with me," said a man named Martin who'd been quiet until now.

"So what do you guys do in here?" I asked.

Michael raised his hand a little then spoke. "It's not unlike the outside. We have cable, and there are sports and meetings of different clubs. AA is big in here. Obviously, church is huge. We have movie nights and card games, but mostly we do what we can to keep busy."

"Really?"

"Yeah. What did you think?"

"I don't know. I suppose I thought life was spent mostly confined or working."

"Yeah, well, there's a lot of that, but when you have time, you want to keep busy so it doesn't get on top of you, ya know?"

"I do."

"And then we have a canteen so that if we are fortunate to have someone on the outside that cares, they send us money and we can buy chips, candy, sandwiches, soda, and personal items."

"What about the guys who don't have any money?"

"They have to work or trade for it."

Sam perked up. "And we get three meals a day, our friends are here, and we get to watch the best shows on TV. Exactly what are we missing? I had to survive on the streets, which is much more difficult and dangerous. But we have a community in here, and we watch each other's backs as best we can."

"What about your freedom?"

"We all miss that," Sam said. "The guards are not exactly good to us, and we miss our friends and family on the outside."

"Johnny?" Dorothy interrupted. "Why don't you pass out some of the Palanca letters?"

Palanca is a Spanish word that means *to give rise, to lift*. Our family, friends, and strangers write Palanca letters to the outsiders and residents, to offer support and guidance in the form of prayer. The message underlying each is that God loves you so much that He moved a person unknown to you to extend His blessing. On a day dedicated to the rise in the form of renewal and rebirth of the residents, Palanca letters are a moving sign of God's love.

Watching the residents read their letters reminded me of receiving letters from Dad while I was at camp. It brought tears to my eyes. Good tears, good memories. Mom was out of my life, and Dad was doing all he could to keep my brother, sister, and me happy and together. Camp and this period of my life was like an island of calm in an otherwise turbulent sea.

It didn't last. The summer Dad remarried, he sent my brother and I back to the camp we'd gone to for years. My sister went to her camp, too. Unlike past summers, only one letter arrived during the first week of the month-long camp. Then nothing until near the end of camp.

That last letter began with the usual "hope you are doing well" but the message soon shifted. "Before you hear it from someone else, your mother is coming back into your life. She bought a house and will move into it in August. As you can imagine, there has been a lot of discussion as to you, your sister, and brother. Your mother wants custody of you all, and so do I. A judge will decide what's best. In fact, a judge has already ordered that the three of you live with your mother and spend every other weekend with Celeste and me.

"Johnny, I can't tell you how sorry I am for this. It's a gut punch, to be sure, but I am optimistic the judge will see the light, so to speak, and make the correct decision for you three and for our family.

"Be well, and have fun, Johnny."

My brother was just seven years old and at camp for the first time in his life. Nothing, and I mean nothing, in his young life was as exciting as being at that camp. When I found him with his tribe of first-timers, his smile, a jumble of oversized adult teeth and small, crooked child's teeth, looked as if it had been etched into his face from too much use.

"She's what?" he asked as his smile faded and was replaced by fear and uncertainty.

"Mom's coming back, and we're going to live with her."

Mom's alcoholism was progressing unabated by any real thoughts of recovery, and within a year, I would abandon my brother and sister with Mom so that I could live with Dad. I have never stopped regretting that decision. I should have stayed with them. They needed me.

###

"COUNT!" screamed a guard.

That is so disruptive, I thought but then understood they had a job to do.

"Line up!" another guard yelled after the residents—now forced back into the reality of their imprisonment—finished their count. "We are off to lunch. Prisoners first then outsiders. Single file, and stay quiet and in line. You may sit with the prisoners in the lunch hall."

I got in line behind Sam.

"You're in for a surprise," he said with a grin.

"Why is that?"

He just chuckled, leaving it to my imagination.

Single file, we left the room and walked to the dining hall. All the while, other prisoners yelled profanity-laced taunts at us from the prison yard. Some stopped what they were doing and advanced toward us. My hands shook, and I realized that despite sports, a canteen, TV, and all the rest of it, prison is a hard, dangerous place to be.

Sam turned his head back toward me. "Their bark is much worse than their bite."

I looked at the men yelling obscenities at us and knew that Sam was lying. He was about five-feet-six-inches tall and probably one-hundred-sixty pounds soaking wet. He was all street smarts and attitude, which worked for him, but this was like nothing I'd ever seen. I turned to look at Dorothy, thinking that for a woman—there were nine women and six men in our group—this must be terrifying. Her face was impassive, serene.

We passed through a doorway, and then the most powerful smell of chemicals, rot, and fetid gruel nearly forced me to my knees. Sam and James looked back at me, laughing.

"I told you," Sam said.

"What?"

"The surprise I told you about."

I didn't know that human food could smell like that. It's indescribable, but a smell I will never forget.

We were the only people in the cafeteria. It would have been too disruptive to have our group of residents and outsiders eating with the rest of the prison population. We stood in line to gather our sporks—a plastic spoon/fork—and trays and proceed through the food line.

First up was salad and bread. I could just live on these, but we were encouraged to eat what the residents eat. I moved down the line.

"What's the gray thing?" I asked the cafeteria worker.

He was pleasant but didn't smile. "Salisbury steak."

"Get tons of gravy," Sam suggested.

"And salt," James added.

The veteran outsiders' plates were filled with salad and bread, including Dorothy's. "I thought we were supposed to eat what the residents eat."

Dorothy crimped her shoulders and said, "It's highly *suggested*."

Hoping I could get closer to my resident team, I looked at Sam and James's trays and did what they did. I loaded up with grays, greens, and whites and didn't try to guess past their colors as to what food they were. And I loaded up with gravy.

A worker chuckled. "A little gravy for your food?"

The residents seemed to have a strategy of eating as quickly as they could lest they taste the food. There was no conversation, so I picked up my spork and dug into the colors. There was nothing fresh about the vegetables nor anything else. The lettuce was at best wilted, the bread stale, and I think the Salisbury steak was from World War II reserves. I thought I might lose everything in my stomach on the first bite, but I endeavored to persevere.

Sam and James smiled at me and then they and the rest of my tablemates started to laugh.

"It took us a while," one of the fellas said.

"Nothing a little Italian dressing couldn't cure," I responded.

Somehow, I made it halfway through the meal then threw in the towel.

"Stuffed," I gasped and began laughing. Note to self: only bread and salad next time.

On our way to our sanctuary, the guards let us stop at a designated smoking area.

"Smoke 'em if you got 'em!" a guard yelled.

I still smoked, so I stepped out with the other residents to cut a butt.

"Really, why are you here, man?" one of the residents asked.

"To be one hundred percent honest with you guys, I'm only recently sober, and Olivia—I know her from AA—asked if I would like to participate in a REC. I had no idea what it was but was willing to try anything anyone suggested, and I agreed. Just like most of you, this is my first, and I'm trying to keep my expectations low, not really knowing what to expect."

"It's hard to get and stay sober," Sam said. "Believe it or not, it's easy to get drugs and alcohol in here."

"Really?" Looking around, it didn't seem easy to get anything other than the snot beat out of you.

"How did you stay sober?" Michael asked.

"I had an epiphany or burning bush early in my sobriety. I wrote a letter and read it in front of my outpatient group. From that moment on, six weeks into sobriety, I haven't had an urge to drink.

"Before I got sober, I nearly died from addiction, but I believe I was saved by God. I was chosen by Him—why, I don't know—but it's my obligation to reach out and help others. When Olivia asked me to do this REC, she told me it would benefit others as well as myself. And here I am."

Sam nodded. "Cool. I bet ninety-five percent of the men in here got into trouble because of drugs and alcohol. AA is pretty big in here, and I've been sober for a little more than a year."

"Good job, man," said a resident. "I got almost nine months."

"January 5, 1999 is my sobriety birthday," I said.

"Mine's August 6, 1998," Sam said.

Then they all chimed in, *I got six months, I got three years, one year, five years* . . . Then one guy arched his back and said, "I got fifteen years." We bowed down to him and started laughing.

"THAT'S ENOUGH!" barked a guard. "Time to go in."

The crazy thing was that, in that moment, I had more in common with those prisoners than the guards. Who would've guessed?

We returned to our sanctuary where Tony led us in singing "Swing Low Sweet Chariot." I knew a lot of the words, even *If I get there before you do, I'll cut a hole and pull you through,* which I'm sure is Lizzy's influence. I remembered her constant mumbling as she shuffled around the kitchen, and every now and then it was punctuated by the verse of a song. I miss her still.

Olivia stepped to the center of the room and said the next talk would be on living a Christian life. Then she turned to James and said, "It's time for you to go prepare in the kitchen, James."

James? I looked toward him, and as he stood, he mumbled, "Man, I'm nervous."

Dorothy's eyes widened. "Nothing to be nervous about, James. You are here among friends, God, and Jesus."

James nodded then disappeared into the kitchen.

This was the ritual for each of the speakers, to be called up by Olivia or Mary Fran and then go to the kitchen for a few minutes. I had no idea why the kitchen and asked Dorothy.

"There is a specially designed prayer group in the kitchen that prays upon the speaker in the hopes that he gives an informative talk and that it is received with open arms and ears."

I nodded my head as if I understood.

James's talk was filled with passion and personal stories, and I felt humbled by the depth of his experiences and his ability to share them with such emotion and clarity. *I could never do what he's just done,* I thought.

When he finished, the room gave him a standing ovation, and he came back to our table to high fives and pats on his back.

"Please discuss James's talk among yourselves," Olivia said.

Sam jumped in first.

"You covered it all, my man. You explained what it is for us to lead a Christian lifestyle and how through knowing, loving, and serving God we can have a relationship with him."

"You really did," I said. "You showed through your story and personal experiences the Christian life of piety and the misconceptions of piety, and how to live a true and authentic life versus the false life we lived before. Nicely done."

When discussion time passed, other residents and outsiders came to James and shared how moved they were by his words. His smile was ear to ear, and probably for the first time in quite a while, there was joy in his heart. And yet, I felt a mild pang of sadness. I believed that I could never move people as he'd done and as I'd seen others do on this weekend and elsewhere.

"COUNT!" yelled a guard.

When the residents returned to their tables, Dorothy announced it was time for chapel visits. As a table, we went to a small, nondescript room off the kitchen area. It was not much bigger than a utility closet, but it was big enough for us to sit in a circle on the floor with a lit candle at the center. There was no other light.

"This is our time to spend with Jesus, either silently or out loud. Please feel free to express your emotions any way you want. You can yell, speak softly or loudly, or remain silent. This is your opportunity to get anything that is bothering you off your chest.

"Christ hears silent and out-loud words. He is your friend and someone you can always trust and turn to in times of need. Please speak your mind and then pass the crucifix to your left. You all will have a turn to speak to our Savior."

Some of the men were truly angry with God and Jesus. They felt as if they'd been ignored or let to suffer when others prospered within their gaze. I didn't take from them a hatred or disbelief in the divine power. It was more like a frustrated and angry child wondering why a parent had let them tumble. Neither Dorothy nor anyone else offered solutions. We remained respectful and silent to let these men work through their relationship with God and Jesus.

Others spoke of how their coming to faith, God, and Jesus changed them and changed their lives. That even as they remained confined behind prison walls, they knew their spirit to be free, and that if they walked God's path and followed Jesus's example, there would be a better life for them in this world and a home for them in the next.

Sam handed the crucifix to me, and for the life of me, I wasn't sure what to say. From somewhere deep within me, within my heart, I thanked Jesus for his sacrifice upon the cross and for dying for our sins, mine included, because the good Lord knows there are many. And then I thanked God for giving me a second chance and lifting me from the cold kitchen floor as I drank myself to death.

"I spent my life trying to fill a God-sized hole within me with alcohol, sex, and drugs, but all I ever found was greater emptiness," I said. "The cure was AA, but the power that got me there was God. And now, I know, truly know, that peace and salvation are more important than money or possessions. I fill the hole within me by serving God and by being of service to others each day, as was taught by Jesus."

These were early days after coming to sobriety and spirituality. I had faith, but it had little form, and I was not an adherent of a religion. I just knew God had lifted me up. But this weekend began a process of awakening to another way of life, a way even fuller and richer than the pink cloud of sobriety.

We returned to our table and waited as the other tables took their turns in the chapel. We were becoming a family. There were jokes and teasing and then weighty conversations that probed a bit deeper into each other's lives and thoughts. The bars and guards, though not completely gone, had faded from view.

The last table emerged from the chapel, and Mary Fran stepped to the center of the room. "Okay, I want everybody to line up along the walls."

We did as she instructed, and the Wheaties emerged from the kitchen with pails of warm soapy water, rags, and towels.

Earlier, before leaving for the REC, Olivia had mentioned to me there would be a surprise as old as Jesus during the REC.

"What? My dad's going to show up?" I laughed.

Olivia frowned a little. "No. It will be one of the most meaningful and humbling experiences you will have in this lifetime."

Mary Fran continued, "This is the service of washing the feet. At the Last Supper, Jesus washed the feet of His disciples. At the time, feet washing was done prior to entering a structure and was considered the lowliest job. It was an act of humility.

"As in John 13:1-16, no servant is greater than his master, nor is a messenger greater than the one who sent him. Washing another's feet means to serve the marginal and give them hope. Even at Easter, the new Pope has been known to go to the local correctional facility and wash the residents' feet.

"Please form eight lines of roughly equal numbers and one by one approach the eight buckets being manned by the outsiders, and when you've had your feet washed, please volunteer and man a bucket and wash the next person in line until all the insiders and outsiders have had their feet washed and washed others' feet."

One by one, we moved through the line. I washed Sam's feet and he, in turn, washed mine. Afterward, we hugged and wished each other peace.

I was forming a deep connection with these men, particularly with Sam. There was compassion and kindness in his eyes. It was hard to imagine that this man had ended up behind bars, and as hard as it was, I forbade myself from inquiring as to the nature of his crime.

I looked at Olivia, and she looked directly into my eyes and smiled. She was witnessing a change in me—and in this room—take place. I'd gone from an egomaniac with an inferiority complex to an individual who served Jesus and the Lord.

It was being proved to me over and over that God had played a huge role in my life despite the fact I continually got in His way. And despite all I'd done and the myriad ways I'd pushed Him from my life, when I called out for him like a child in the dark on January 5, 1999, he obliged, even knowing I would probably fail Him again.

Before the REC weekend, the notion of Jesus, his death to atone for my sins, and the knowledge that he walks with me was just that—a distant notion, its image blurred and unrecognizable. But now, a slight crack within my heart and mind allowed me to see with clarity. Life wasn't working before I became sober and gained my faith, so why not try trusting?

I accepted Jesus into my life in that moment. "Thank you, Jesus, and thank you, God, for my incredible life. I won't let you down again." A tear ran down my cheek, and I looked up, embarrassed by being so transparent.

Sam smiled at me and seemed to know exactly what had just happened. "God is great. Jesus is great. Welcome, brother."

The tears then flowed. All those years of drinking to fill a God-sized hole, and here, in prison, a place I'd feared more than any other, the hole was filled to overflowing.

Why didn't I try this years ago, find God, find Jesus? I thought. *Why did I have to go through so much pain to get to this point of pure love and jubilation? Why hadn't Mom found this? More importantly, why did I have to inflict so much pain on others? Without question, I am as hardheaded as they come. For me to learn anything new or change, I must go through incredible pain. Why?*

The answer that came to me in that moment, and the answer that remains, is that everyone is pretty much in the same boat. It takes almost dying to truly change. Without authentic fear, without seeing across the thin vapor between life and death into the horizon just beyond the horizon, change rarely takes place. God gives us that view as we fall, and if we let him, he will catch us.

COUNT!

The residents lined up and then returned to the tables. Olivia stepped to the center of the room. "Alright, friends, if the residents will go to the kitchen, we have a very special surprise for you."

They stood, and we outsiders unpacked tablecloths, candles, and utensils, which we'd received permission from the warden to bring in. The room wasn't The Ritz, but it was a fine dining hall for our catered meal, which was barbecued ribs, chicken, and pork with salads, potatoes, fresh vegetables, and soda, followed by cake.

The residents' smiles and hugs of thanks were incredible. This was the best meal many had seen in years, and we were happy to provide it for them. All one had to do was open their eyes to know that God was here, too.

Sam finished his plate and then disappeared into the kitchen. When he returned, he held two plates of cake and handed one to me. "Let me serve you," he said, and I smiled.

After polishing off the cake, the room sort of fell into a stunned silence, broken only by murmurs of conversation and praise for the meal.

"COUNT! And leave the utensils on the table so they can be collected and counted to be sure none of you pocketed anything!" a guard yelled.

The rest of the evening was filled with skits, and some of the residents stood before the room to give witness to God's presence in their lives. Their honesty was impressive and inspiring, but still, I wondered, as with James's talk, if I could be so open and able to move others with my words and presence as these men could.

And then, it was over.

"LINE UP!" a guard yelled.

We hugged and said our goodnights to the residents and watched them march back into the world they must inhabit. The sanctuary was quiet, and I missed them.

"Great day, everyone, and thank you," Olivia said. "Please clean up and pack up. It's ten, and the guards are ready to be done with the day."

Though it was a long day and a moonless night outside the van, inside we were a lively group, laughing and trading stories of things that happened during the day. When we arrived back at the motel, Olivia pulled me aside.

"I could see a change in you, Johnny Lipscomb, and I just wanted to make sure you're okay."

My eyes welled as I spoke. "I could see myself in these men. They're just as human and fallible as any one of us, but I've seen them go through so much change over the last couple of days that I've found myself wanting what they had."

That didn't make any sense, but those men had something that I have never been able to grasp. A true and sincere belief in something greater than themselves. They were willing to trust one hundred percent that everything was going to be okay and that their past sins would be forgiven. Despite my awakening to Jesus and his role in my life, I didn't have the confidence in myself that those men in prison had.

Olivia looked up at me. I could see in her eyes how tired she was, yet her will was still there, pushing her along. "I have watched you since day one when you came into AA. I chose you to be in this REC for a reason. Since the letter that you wrote your mother, there has been a drastic change in your demeanor. You have willingness, you help others, you are accountable, and you have compassion for yourself and others.

"I have watched you, Johnny, and believe me, this is the case for you. We don't see the change in ourselves at first—others do.

"You should also remember that those men have a tremendous amount of time to work on themselves, and what is clear is that it works for them. You're new to this sober way of life, and it's going to take you a while to figure it all out, but I have faith you are in it for the long term."

She patted my shoulder, and in her touch, I felt a mother's presence, a woman who cared enough to offer support when I needed it and a reprimand when I overstepped the mark.

She pulled me closer. "The percentage of those staying sober for a year is somewhere between five to ten percent, and I don't usually pick someone with less than a year to do a REC, but there is something different about you.

"You have enough to think about, so let's say goodnight. Get some sleep and get ready for our final day."

I hugged Olivia, thanked her, then headed to my room where I closed the door and got on my knees. I prayed before God and Jesus to thank them for this life and the opportunity to be of service.

The alarm woke me at six-thirty. Same process. Quick shower, coffee, pastry, then into a van. This day was a little different because my mind and body felt spent, but in a good way.

We arrived at the prison and went through the usual security procedure to get back to our sanctuary. Olivia stood in the middle of the room. "I know you all are beat, but let's give this last day a big push, okay?"

The little titan had spoken, and it wasn't a question she was asking.

The third day is *Go Forth* day and is taken from Matthew 28:18-20 in which Jesus says, "*As the Father has sent me, so I send you.*" Go forth is a request from God that the residents continue the road they've started down, and if they fail, to stand back up, brush themselves off, and continue again. And as they travel this path, they are to share the message of Christ with others because when we grow, we all grow.

We replaced the posters from the day before with ones encouraging the residents to keep with the path. In the kitchen, the cooks and servers got busy cutting and pouring. The guards looked a little more at ease, but I stress, a little more.

As with the two days before, we heard the heavy, rubbery steps of the residents as they approached the door to the sanctuary. But unlike the first day, and even more so than the second day, they were in high spirits. Rather than voiceless footsteps, there was laughing, talking in loud voices, and camaraderie that we could sense through the door. When they came through, there were smiles on everyone's faces.

Tony launched into "Glory in My Redeemer" on his guitar, and without much encouragement, we all joined in. Afterward, one of the Wheaties called out, "Coffee and donuts are on the way!"

"COUNT OFF!" was the reply from a guard.

The men lined up and performed their count as trays of donuts and coffee were set at each table. As soon as the count finished, they were on it like white on rice. We outsiders joined in, too.

Mary Fran spoke on the topic of Go Forth, saying, "What is past is past. You must support and be supported. Share your newfound life with others, reach out, and pass on the good word of Jesus our Lord and Savior."

A chorus of praise Jesus and amen rose from the room.

Following her brief talk, we asked the residents at our table what they planned to do with this information.

Michael said, "I'm going to start a prayer group."

James said, "I think I'm going to start a hospice group. Many of the residents die in here each year, and they have nobody."

Sam said, "I may study to become a minister and pass the good word on. Tend to my flock as they say."

When we finished, there was the Bible Enthronement Ceremony, a discussion of God in our relationships, and a resident spoke on God and the life of an inmate.

Throughout, the chorus broke in with "Praise Jesus" or "Amen" when the spirit moved them, which was often.

"COUNT AND LINE UP FOR LUNCH!" yelled a guard, and I couldn't believe the time had gone so quickly. The count was done, and we walked to the cafeteria where I and the other outsiders basically held our noses and choked the food down. Lots of salt, gravy, and ketchup.

"I feel for you guys," I said to Sam and James as I tried to force down a piece of meat, the provenance of which was indeterminate as was its age.

"After the first hundred meals, it gets a lot better," James said.

Back in the sanctuary, Tony walked from table to table taking photos. James, Michael, and Sam stood behind and around me for our photos. I was honored.

There was a talk by one of the resident cooks on how to transition from this weekend experience back into the regular prison routine. He recommended keeping in touch with the fellow residents in the room and getting involved with other programs offered at the prison, or, if possible, creating a new one.

He ended with, "Change daily from what you used to do. There's a lot going on here if you look for it."

We sang another hymn then the cooks announced another snack was on its way, which was followed by the command to do a count by a guard. Then Mary Fran stepped to the center of the room.

"It is now time for the final liturgy. Our time here will be over shortly, and this is probably the last time our whole group will be together."

With her words, the room fell silent. You could hear a pin drop. The men realized that they would be on their own in a little while.

"Go forth with the Lord. Grow in your love of the Lord and give it away to keep it."

Somehow, Sam got separated from the table when we began to sing "Peace is Flowing Like a River." I looked around the room and saw him on the other side, his back against a wall. He saw me, too, and walked around the edge of the room and put his arm around my shoulder. We sang from the hymnal.

A tear fell from my eye. How did I become so attached to a prisoner, a man locked away for a crime I knew nothing about, only that it was serious enough to land him here for years? *Praise Jesus, I* thought. *You are powerful and almighty.*

Bread and grape juice for wine were brought to the altar, and one by one the residents and outsiders received the sacrament. Off to the side, Olivia stood at a table with cards signed by the outsiders wishing the residents well, crosses, and the pictures taken earlier. The men picked up their items and gave Olivia a last hug.

My chest tightened as I looked around our table at Michael, James, Sam, and the rest of them. I knew this would likely be the last time I would see them.

"LINE UP! PREPARE TO MOVE OUT!"

There was not a dry eye in our sanctuary. Hugs were exchanged, thanks were expressed, and we hoped to see each other in a month for the scheduled reunion.

Then they marched out of the sanctuary back into prison, back to guards and others seeing them as prisoners or inmates rather than the men they were.

I had to sit down to compose myself. When the residents started to sing "God is Amazing," a favorite from the weekend, it was all I could do not to bawl like a baby.

The song faded, and the door shut hard behind the last man.

Later, I climbed into my car. It was an early fall evening, the colors still ablaze and the air fresh, clean. I drove with the top of the car up, no music, in silence. When I got home, it was too quiet.

CHAPTER 7
I AM A LIAR, THIEF, ADULTERER, CHEATER

THE MORNING AFTER the REC, I rose with the sun, showered, ate a small breakfast, then drove to my morning AA meeting. Olivia was there, looking a little tired, with some of my newfound friends. I suppose we all looked a little peaked, yet energized and somehow different for the experience of the REC.

I couldn't help but think about Sam, Michael, James, and the other residents I got to know. Had they been as deeply affected as I was or were they staring at yet another plate of horrid colors and just thinking about getting through the day? I hoped that our shared experience was enough to help ease the remainder of their time, if not change their lives.

On the drive to the meeting, I thought about what the experience meant to me and how I should use it in my life. As well as being physically spent, I was also emotionally spent. Prior to the REC, Olivia had told me to take a few days off afterward to rest and sit with all I'd learned and experienced. Contemplate how I felt and see if I could sense any change within me.

I suppose the first thing I noticed was that I felt exhausted, but in a good way. As if I'd accomplished something important for someone else. This led me to a question: *Who helped whom?*

As I teased that around my mind, I remembered Monday mornings before sobriety. Waking up feeling like a bus hit me and I ate a skunk then racing to the fridge for a beer. Friends would ask about my weekend, and usually all I could muster was "You wouldn't believe it" and left it at that. If they asked now? "You wouldn't believe it, but I went to prison and helped about sixty residents encounter Christ."

They probably would have asked Dad to lock me up.

As usual, Olivia was toward the front of the room, but when she saw me, she walked over and asked, "How are you feeling, Johnny?"

"Absolutely beat."

"Me too. I always do after the REC weekends. It usually takes me a week to recover."

Olivia has a terrible back and is about fifteen years older than I am, but in the REC, she didn't complain one wit and had more energy than anyone in the room.

"How do you do it?" I asked. "I was tired the whole weekend, both emotionally and physically."

"It lifts me up, Johnny. It's what I live for. The prison ministry is a big part of my program."

"What program?"

"My AA program. There are many ways to get and stay sober, and giving back to the prison ministry is one of my paths to continue my sobriety. I also take AA meetings to prison, have quilting groups with the residents, started a garden club, and a few other things."

"Impressive."

"I just want to stay sober and have a good life. This works, so why change?"

"It certainly shows. It's an honor to know you, Olivia."

She smiled and gently held my arm with one hand. "You are going to go a long way in this program, Johnny. I have watched you over the past few months, and the growth in you is incredible. You appear to have the qualities to be a leader and to be able to connect with others on a deeper level."

She had obviously misread me. I'm a liar, thief, con man, adulterer, and cheater. I look out for myself first and don't care who I hurt. She would figure that out.

She must have read something in my eyes that caused her to step back but speak in a soothing, motherly voice. "Try to get some rest the next few days before you resume your work schedule. Take the time to think and meditate about the weekend and what it meant and more importantly where you go from here with it.

"I also want to thank you for your participation. You were a huge help and an inspiration to the residents. There will be a reunion, you know? In about a month at the correctional facility. Are you in?"

"Absolutely."

I did as she suggested and took a few days off. My hidden dog fence business was starting to really grow, and being fall, it was usually busy. I'd brought it from the brink of collapse to where it was now, thriving and taking up much of my time, but I loved it. There was rarely anyone to bother me as I worked, and I got to talk with dogs most days. There are no better creatures on this earth than dogs. They live in the moment, and if treated with kindness and patience, they give unconditional love.

Installing fences on my own all day gave me time to think and reflect on the REC weekend.

I decided to continue this spiritual journey and search out other means of obtaining what I'd felt during the REC and then in the days and weeks following. I started trying new churches. Unity Church in St. Louis was close to the outpatient twelve-step program I'd attended, so I started there. It did help me feel closer to God, but it didn't give me that huge rush that the sweat lodges or the REC provided.

I started meditating, which I found difficult and abandoned after a week. I wasn't yet at a serene-enough place in my program to fully understand and appreciate meditation. In a few years, it would play a crucial role in my life, but not now.

I also started attending new AA meetings. By then, I was going to two or three meetings per day, seven days a week. With the meetings, I began to read spiritual material, continued working the AA steps with my sponsor, and sponsored my first AA member. I made coffee, brought donuts, and did what I could to be of service at a few of my meetings.

I knew that all these activities were good to do. They were the right and polite thing. I also had a sense that in some way they worked, perhaps subconsciously, to further my recovery. But it wasn't until reflecting on each of these as I dug the trench for a hidden dog fence that I recognized a connection to what Olivia said about her pathways.

Each action I took to improve myself or serve another worked in conjunction as a pathway for my program. Some were for me, and some for others. Compassion for myself and compassion for others. Some provided a bigger lift and growth like the REC and sweat lodges, but all of them were my program. This was why I had been successful so far, and each combined to form a path for me to follow.

Follow the yellow brick road! Follow the yellow brick road to find my way home, just like in the *Wizard of Oz*, one of my favorite movies.

During the month before the REC reunion, I did another sweat lodge and relayed my REC experience to my lodge brothers. They were amazed and intrigued.

And the pink cloud continued.

The month passed quickly, and on a cold, early winter day I rode with Olivia out to Farmington. Along the way we talked, and she told me her story of coming to AA. It's her story to tell, so I won't do it here, but suffice it to say, all I could think was, *What a brave soul.*

We pulled into the prison parking lot. Everything around seemed to be some hue of gray—the pavement, the building, the clouds above. Everything had a downcast aura to it.

Not all the outsiders were able to attend. The RECs take up a considerable amount of time, which includes the preparation over three or four Saturdays, the weekend, and then decompressing after it is all over. Most people don't have the time to include a reunion, though I was happy to see that a few of us were able to make it.

The guards took a photo of each of us and created a visitor tag that we wore around our necks. They then led us through the building and yard to the stark room that had been our sanctuary. Without the posters, residents, and the frenetic activity of the REC, and with fewer outsiders, the room felt completely different. It replicated the grayness outside more than being the sanctuary it once was and the place where so many had experienced so much.

I didn't like being there and wanted to leave.

We heard the same clumping of rubber-soled shoes, chattering, and guards yelling as we had the month before, but when the door opened, only about half of the insiders came through. Hugs and greetings were exchanged, and with that, the air inside the room changed a bit. The men were friendly enough, but their guard was up, and the ice wall we'd broken through a month ago returned. We had only two hours, so I assumed there would not be time to break through again.

Of my tablemates, James was the only one to come to the reunion.

"Where are Sam and Michael?" I asked James.

"Don't know. After the REC, most of the guys fell back into their old way of life in here."

Hearing that disappointed and saddened me. I thought the four of us—James, Sam, Michael, and me—had made a lasting connection.

We spoke with the other residents, had a few laughs, and it was evident that those who did come were happy to see us. They explained how for a few days the residents from the REC stayed together, ate together, and prayed together, but then one or two fell away until there were only a few of them left.

I looked into James's eyes and then to the other residents, and within them, I recognized that we did have an effect. God had touched all of us over that weekend. For these men, it was enough to keep them on the path, and I should be thankful for that.

Since entering recovery, I've recognized what I consider to be undeniable truths about life. I do believe that unless someone hits a life or death crossroads, it is virtually impossible for that person to change. Most of the time, seeing into death is not enough. Mom confronted the failure of her life and death more times than I will probably know, but it was never enough to bring her back. I've never known the kind of woman she was. Who was it that resided deep within her alcohol-rattled mind and body? Where did what I assume to be a scared little girl hide away? She never gave me or my sister or brother any clues. We heard stories from older family—she was a beautiful and kind young woman, we were told—but we never could experience that woman.

Why was I able to change? Why was I chosen and not her? These thoughts haunt me to this day.

But as I chatted and laughed with these men, I recognized change. I saw it within them and thought that perhaps, like me, something bored down deep enough into their hearts, minds, and souls to wake them up and keep them awake to God. Further, I believed that I played a part, a small part, in helping that happen. It was proof that being chosen is a blessing and an obligation. Sobriety, love, and a happy life are some of the blessings that came to me, but the obligation was to do as Jesus did. Be of service to whomever I come across and don't be surprised by whose life changes by it. I'd love to have seen Sam and Michael, but James was there as well as about twenty others. May they find the blessings I've found.

We said our goodbyes, walked out of the facility, heard the lock for the last time, and I thanked God once again.

Olivia and I sat in silence as we drove home. I had a lot to think about.

###

I continued to grow in the program of Alcoholics Anonymous over the next year. I sponsored a few more people, kept up with my meetings, worked the steps, and tried to be of service wherever I could.

At the same time, I participated in more sweat lodges, grew my social circle, and engaged more with my family. I also did what I could to reestablish a relationship with my son and daughter, but nothing I did brought us closer. The memory of backing the car out of the driveway to go drink and cheat on their mom and looking up to see their beautiful little faces in the window staring out at me is more than I can bear. For a long time, I thought it was my burden alone. As I grew in my sobriety and began to work the long-atrophied emotions of empathy and sympathy, I started to see beyond myself and through the eyes of others. With this, came the realization that my children carry that memory and many others with them. If I could not excise that memory and its searing pain from my mind and spirit, it must also live within my children.

One night, as I turned these thoughts in my head, the phone rang.

"Johnny, it's Olivia. How would you like to do another REC with me?"

"I'm sorry, Olivia, I just don't have the time."

"Please make time. I know you will get a lot out of it."

"I just can't.

"It's at a women's correctional facility in Vandalia, and I promise it will be a completely different experience from Farmington."

"I don't know, Olivia."

"Have I ever led you down the wrong road? Please, Johnny."

"I don—"

"Johnny, please."

"Okay, okay. When is it?"

"Two months, and I want you to be a table leader, and I want you to give one of the talks."

"January?"

"Yes."

"Okay, let's do it."

"Thank you so much."

"You're welcome. You know I can't turn you down."

"Johnny, you would not be turning me down. You would be turning down the residents."

I hung up the phone and thought, *Wait a minute. Did she say I was giving a talk?*

It was the first Saturday of December that our new REC team got together for the first time and received our assignments. Mary Fran was the director of this REC. While my respect and love for Olivia knew no bounds, I was becoming increasingly fond of Mary Fran and her calm, gentle way. Without a change in tone or expression, she got things accomplished.

As Olivia had warned, I was to head table ten, which would have nine female residents, but no observer as I had done at our table during the first REC for Dorothy. This alone was enough to make me nervous, but added to it was the assignment to give the talk on *Christian Ideals and Christian Maturity*. This was to be one of the first talks given over the three days.

"Johnny," Mary Fran said, "both Olivia and I are confident you can do a good job with this talk, which is why I've assigned it to you. Just remember, it's the first talk of the REC, so it must break the ice with the residents as well as be lively and to the point. Okay?"

"I can do it," I said, but I wasn't so sure.

Before disbanding the first organizing meeting, Mary Fran said we should prepare our talks so they could be critiqued at the next meeting, a week away.

As I drove home, I thought about the responsibility handed to me. I was not a great public speaker and to date had rarely strayed far from speaking on my recovery story, something I knew well. *How in the world am I going to weave my story of personal growth with the Christian ideals and how to reach them?* I wondered. *Am I even qualified?*

I sat at my computer and started to think and write. This would be *Die Day*, so it must be serious without bringing the whole room down. Fortunately, there was an outline I could follow, so I worked through that list:

What were your ideals as a child?

I would grow up and be a successful businessman.

What were your ideals as a teenager?

Not much different, except that I would have a family and be wealthy.

What did you expect your adulthood to be like?

I expected to achieve my child and teenage ideals.

When you were a child/teenager, where, if anywhere, did God, church, and the sacraments fit?

Easiest one so far, I thought. God, church, and the sacraments had no place in my life. We were not expected nor encouraged to attend church. Religion was never discussed in our household.

Now that you are an adult, where do God, church, and the sacraments fit? Is this a change? Why?

I knew I had to be honest with the residents and outsiders, so I wrote, "Church and the sacraments are not part of my life." To this point in my recovery, I'd sought out different churches to help fill that hole in my life, but I hadn't found one. The only one that even came close was Unity Church where the teachings were close to a twelve-step program.

As a young adult, God didn't hold a place in my heart or mind, but that drastically changed when I got sober. I fully believed in God and knew He existed in my life. How I knew that was rather simple: I had changed. I prayed to God multiple times each day, but it took a long time for me to get past the idea that I should expect results from God for these prayers. I prayed for His wisdom and constantly searched for His will for me.

Even to this day, I am only one hundred percent sure of two things. It is God's will that I stay sober, and it is God's will that I help others. I may never find another truth, but I know these two for sure, and I try my best at both. Maybe at some point, my attitude and views toward church will change, but for the time being, AA and sweat lodges work very well at connecting me to my higher power whom I refer to as God.

I don't believe this is how it should work for everybody. For many, church and the sacraments accomplish the same needs as AA and sweat lodges do for me. This is how I pray and connect, and they both teach me how to pray and connect.

What is your personal ideal?

I thought for a moment before writing but quickly came to the notion that St. Nick, a nickname for a friend, was an example of an ideal person. He was a driver for Coca-Cola, and I'd never met someone as content as him. He was ten years sober as I worked through the outline, and yet every time I saw him, he was on a pink cloud. He had a simple job, was extremely grateful for his faith and sobriety, gave one-hundred-percent credit to God, sponsored others, helped lots and lots of people, and was a great family man.

He loved his sober life, and he had a sense of Buddha-like equanimity I'd rarely ever seen. At one AA meeting, he spoke about a close friend dying from an overdose. Although he was devastated by the loss, he talked about how fortunate he was to have known such a fine person. No anger or resentment. He was at peace.

Have your goals changed and matured?

Definitely. When I was an active alcoholic, all I cared about was myself, and that usually involved material possessions. I had a huge ego while at the same time suffering from an inferiority complex, if that makes sense. I would walk over anybody and anything to get what I wanted, and I did just that. I hurt so many innocent people in my life, and the worst was the pain I caused my innocent children.

Today, I can slide back into that frame of mind if I am not centered spiritually. The list is long, but suffice it to say, I am making living amends for all those years of living a dishonest, deceitful life.

How has God's presence in your life altered or shaped your adult ideal?

Once I came to believe in the existence of God and how he saved my life when I couldn't do it on my own, I tried to do what I believed was God's will. Not that it is always evident, but I try the best I can.

How much and what are you willing to sacrifice to fulfill God's purpose for your life?

As stated above, I believe God's will for me is to stay sober and to help others. I'm not so sure it is a sacrifice, but I go to as many AA meetings as possible, work the steps, work with others, follow my sponsor's advice, and keep looking for opportunities to help others.

That was the last question in the outline, and with that, I constructed what I believed to be a decent talk.

At the next planning meeting, Mary Fran stood in the middle of the room. "Okay, Johnny, go ahead and read your talk."

I felt the back of my neck tense, and my jaw stiffened as I read, and then I let out a sigh of relief as I finished. My ego was still lost in the past. I thought I had killed it. But then I looked at the twenty or so team members, and they were not impressed. A few got up to get coffee or something to eat. Others fidgeted.

"Really good first attempt," Mary Fran said. "Now, go back and make it livelier and to the point. Show how your youth and teen ideals have died and how you have achieved your goals in adulthood. The residents are still not sure what a REC is at this point, so start to explain what the REC experience is all about without putting them to sleep or offending them."

A few others offered constructive criticism and ideas on how to revise it. At first, my ego took a big hit, but with each comment, I became aware that this wasn't about me. This was about helping others and not how I looked or that my first effort wasn't my best. Put the shoe on the other foot and see how my talk would be perceived by the residents. They don't care about the actual results in my life. They need to know or want to know how I got here. What was my journey, and who lit the path?

I took their suggestions to heart and rewrote the talk and learned the lesson I was meant to receive. What I consider important, others in different situations probably couldn't care less about. I heard one time that what you say is interesting, but what I say is important. I had to reverse that thinking. What you say is important, and maybe

I can add something interesting to it. Probably the best foundation I know of to be a true friend.

A few years before, I would have been irate that something I put so much effort into was criticized. But I learned that the criticism isn't important. What's important is how the residents hear and react to my talk.

As our van approached the women's correctional center in Vandalia, I started to get that queasy lump in my throat again. Barbed wire has a way of doing that to me. The building was once again nondescript, dull, and ominous, just like at Farmington.

January can be an exceptionally cold month in Missouri, and this one was no different. Christmas and New Year's Eve were behind us, and most folks were waiting for the spring thaw. The wintry chill on this day provided no comfort that spring was coming anytime soon. It was cold and gray from ground to sky, and the forecast called for a few inches of snow.

Through my work in AA, I've become acutely aware of some of my character defects. There is a phrase we use called HALT: Hungry, Angry, Lonely, and Tired. Do your best not to fall into one of these or some combination of these categories because they weaken resilience. I do okay with the first three, but being tired is a huge issue. If I let myself become too tired, I act as if I was drinking. I have zero patience or tolerance and am unpleasant to be around. So I go to bed earlier and take naps, whatever it takes not to become tired.

The other thing I've learned is that I become depressed in winter. Perhaps it's from Christmases past, which were unpleasant, or the weather, but I know that as soon as I hear the first Christmas carol in November, a dark shadow comes over me. It's a little better in sobriety, but it still happens. I had that depressed feeling going into Vandalia.

Of course, the rest of the REC team was in a light mood. Except for two or three additions, it was the same team as Farmington, and each person was talkative, excited, and seemed as if they couldn't care less how gray and cold it was outside.

We went through the same routine at the entrance as at Farmington, and the inside of Vandalia was the exact same as Farmington, except for the fact that the residents were women. There were bland, neutral colors, guard towers, barbed wire, and cool to cold guards—more men than women—who spoke loudly or shouted instructions.

As we walked toward the room that we would turn into our sanctuary, a resident shouted, "Hey, pretty boy."

"Wanna date?" another yelled.

They were laughing and looking at me. I'm sure I turned bright red. I'm not used to that kind of attention.

"Looks like you have some admirers," Mary Fran said.

I gave a half-hearted smile and thought about what it must be like for her and the other women to enter a men's prison.

We turned a corner and entered our new weekend sanctuary. Similar room and size, and a guard barked out directions. "No inappropriate touching. When we say count, please remain seated while we count the prisoners. When we say time to go to meals, please line up single file with the prisoners at the front. Do not exchange phone numbers, addresses, or make any promises. We will be outside these doors, but watching you all very carefully. Do not hesitate to ask questions, especially if you see anything suspicious.

"Thank you."

Like busy bees, we remodeled the room into something resembling a makeshift church with the theme of *Die Day*. The banners were dark, and the mood changed from lightheartedness to a more somber tone. By 9 a.m., we were ready.

Mary Fran gave directions for the weekend once again, and Tony, our music director, played a hymn in the corner of the room on his guitar. I believe it was "Be Thou My Vision."

A moment or two later, we heard the residents approaching. A constant and growing hum came from the other side of the door. I couldn't quite figure out what the humming was, but as they neared, it was clear it was one incessant conversation between about eighty residents.

As with the men, the women residents were every skin tone, size, and shape.

Mary Fran welcomed them in and told them to find their name at their assigned table and then to please take a seat. Every word was respectful and polite. As if Mary Fran were welcoming in a handful of sisters for tea.

I stood by my table and soon introduced myself to Nancy, Linda, Mary, Alondra, Camilla, Maria, Mary Ann, and Lesley. They immediately started playing twenty questions with me, and I was overwhelmed. As much as I like to talk and believe I can chat up any woman, I was a nervous, shy man among these women. I felt like I was twelve years old again—bright red and trying to remain calm.

"Okay, okay, settle down," Mary Fran said. "How about a quick prayer to guide us on the weekend and then a song followed by the Bible Enthronement?"

She chose Philippians 1:9-11. "And this is my prayer: That your love may abound more and more in knowledge and depth of insight, so that you may be able to discern what is best and may be pure and blameless for the day of Christ, filled with the fruit of righteousness that comes through Jesus Christ, to the glory and praise of God."

A chorus of Amen filled the room.

From there, Mary Fran explained the purpose of *Die Day* and then we discussed its meaning among the tables. All nine sets of eyes at my table were on me, and the questions and interrogation continued. They wanted to know everything about me, and I had to work hard to keep turning the direction of the conversation back to the meaning of *Die Day*.

It was abundantly obvious that these women wanted to talk. They opened up in minutes if not seconds. Some were shyer, but all in all, they wanted this to be a social occasion with me as the topic of conversation.

"COUNT!" yelled a guard.

Mary Fran approached me. "Johnny, it's time for you to go to the kitchen to prepare for your talk." Then she smiled and shooed me away.

My palms started to sweat, a lump formed in my throat, and I felt far beyond my comfort zone. I'd spoken quite a few times in AA, but this was something different. It was clear that these women would not hold back if they didn't like what I said. I felt alone and disturbingly transparent to them.

I also had never been into the kitchen as a speaker preparing to give a talk and had no idea what they did in there. One of the insider cooks told me to get on my knees and bow my head while the other cooks and servers gathered around me. I felt their hands on my shoulders, head, and upper body. Then a woman started to pray.

"God, look over this man. Let him speak Your truth. Let him be Your vessel to deliver Your message. Allow the residents to hear Your word of die today and change today. Be not scared in the presence of Your son, Jesus Christ."

Tears filled my eyes, and I started to shake. I'd never felt such physical, emotional, and spiritual connection in one moment as I did then. What had happened?

"Amen," they all said, and I rose to hugs.

They led me out to the altar and then left me there, alone in front of the residents and outsiders.

I cleared my throat and thought to reach for a glass of water, but my hand shook so much that I worried I'd spill the water as I raised it to my lips. I started to speak, but my throat was tight, and I cleared it again and began my talk in almost a whisper.

"My name is Johnny Lipscomb, and I am an alcoholic."

"Hi, Johnny," was their response. A few women shifted in their seats. Some leaned their chins on their knitted fingers and stared at me.

Okay, I thought, *I can do this. I'll treat it like an AA meeting where I am among friends, nobody judging.*

I looked at my text and began.

There is always the talk you want to give, the talk you gave, and the talk you wish you gave. I've learned that if I come close to all three, then I've done my job. I think my talk fit those criteria.

I mixed my story with the topic of *Christian Ideals and Maturity.* I kept it upbeat, but not so that it did not reflect the nature of *Die Day.* I explained the importance of my evolution, how I had to die to change. Some of that was dying from my childhood into adulthood, and some of it was dying from my addiction into recovery.

I also explained that my life is given to me through God's grace, and it is my job to follow His will for me. I explained what I thought God's will was and how I went about it each day—by reaching out and helping others, hence the reason I was there that day. I hit on how I got sober and how I maintained my sobriety. Sometimes, especially early on, it was an hourly battle, occasionally white-knuckling it moment to moment.

I ended my talk with the hope that I'd put these women—most of whom were unfamiliar with what a REC is—at ease and prepared for the remainder of the day and evening.

The women applauded, and when I returned to my table, my tablemates gave me a big hug. That felt great.

I noticed the guard's eyes perk up as the women hugged me, but as far as I was concerned, I had a table full of friends, not threats. I believed I passed the residents' test, and for the remainder of the weekend, I was one of them.

The rest of the weekend went off without a hitch. I became close to the residents at my table, which was wonderful but made saying goodbye to them hard. We sang one last song, hugged tightly, and our eyes welled with tears.

As our team drove away from Vandalia, I looked in my notebook, and on the back page there was a heart with Linda and Maria's names. I showed Olivia.

"Johnny Lipscomb, I have heard enough of your story, and do not try to reach out to them now or in the future. Once we do the REC reunion, move on. It's over."

"Yes, ma'am."

I looked up and thanked God he had chosen me to pass His love on to others. I thanked Him for saving my life and for saving me from incarceration.

I had no idea what would come next, but I had faith that God would show me the path. I just had to keep my eyes open for His signals.

CHAPTER 8
SIGNS

OVER THE NEXT COUPLE of years, I threw myself completely and without reservation into my business. I sold and installed as many hidden dog fences as I possibly could and loved what I did. I was outside, with dogs, and I enjoyed the dirt on my hands and the way my muscles felt at the end of a long day.

The result was that I brought my business from the brink of collapse to something that resembled success. I think Dad, the consummate businessman, was even impressed that I'd managed to turn a small, struggling hidden fence business into a successful, modest-sized enterprise.

Though work was my new God, AA remained an important second God. I sponsored more and more people, kept up with meetings, participated in interventions, spoke to families, and was helping others find solutions rather than creating the problem. I also was speaking more and more at AA meetings and outside of AA. The highlight was telling my story to a graduate class at Washington University where a good friend was a professor.

Life kept getting better, and problems dissipated. The only problem and heartache that I could not resolve despite my attempts to make amends was my relationship with my children. They were closed to me, and the pain of that loss and memories of how I'd hurt them never faded.

Sweat lodges remained part of my sobriety practice. One of the most intense was the weekend after the September 11, 2001 terrorist attacks. A handful of our lodge brothers were veterans, and they had a difficult time dealing with the attacks and their consequences. Many still suffered from PTSD, and the images of the planes hitting the towers and then collapsing gave them flashbacks to things they'd seen in Vietnam.

George, our sweat lodge water pourer recognized that some were suffering and called for a lodge. The veterans shared their experiences, cried, and, I believe, healed a little bit. We sang, prayed to our ancestors, and asked for help to get through what felt like a new way of life. It was also the longest lodge we've ever done. Most lodges last for four doors—a Native American term—but we went through sixteen doors.

I was a different person when I left that day. From seeing my veteran brothers share their thoughts and experiences, I learned a little better what people go through in war and how it affects their civilian life. I felt for these men and thanked God I was never involved in an armed conflict. It also made me realize how lucky I'd been and what an incredible life I had. For me to whine about life— which I did quite a bit before sobriety and a bit after—was nothing but selfish.

Despite all my work, my character defects did not disappear. I could still be impatient, lack balance in life, be judgmental and overly opinionated—and there are a dozen more I could list.

I should put an emphasis on *lacking balance in life*. All these good things happened over the span of about two years, but then I let work become my new God. We alcoholics are broken people who use compulsions to alleviate stress and imbalance. My business grew at an even more rapid pace, and it became all-consuming.

Money fell into my bank account, and I felt a surge of respectability and achievement I'd never experienced.

But it came with a cost. I didn't have time to continue with the RECs, slacked off on my AA schedule, declined to sponsor a couple of people, said no to a few sweat lodges, and ran short on time for everything that had saved my life, including God. I could feel this, that I was letting things—business success and accumulation of money—get between me and God and sobriety. I didn't fully recognize it at the time, but I started to disconnect from myself and think in ways that in the past led to alcohol.

The most notable symptom of my slide was that even when I made it to an AA meeting, I did all I could to sneak out the door when it ended. There were hidden dog fences to install and sell.

"Hey! Johnny Lipscomb, can I speak with you?" Olivia yelled out at the end of one meeting.

"Sure, I have a few minutes."

"I don't see you anymore. How come?"

"Work, Olivia, just work."

"Be careful not to let work take over your life."

"I know, I know—"

"I have an opportunity for you."

Here it comes, I thought to myself.

"Let's sit over here. Do you have a few minutes?"

I was already running behind, but I had to hear what she wanted to say.

"We are doing another REC in a couple months."

"I don't have time, Olivia. Do you need a donation to help with food and supply costs?"

"No. I know you're busy, but I believe this REC is exactly what you need right now."

"I don't know, Olivia. What I need right now is an eighth day in the week."

She frowned then said, "It's in April at the Potosi, Missouri Men's Correctional Facility."

"I'm sure it will be wonderful, but I don't have the time, especially in April when it's the busiest time of the year for me."

"You'll get a ton out of it."

"I wish I could, but there is no way. Thanks for thinking of me."

I started to get up and give her a hug when she whispered, "It's for residents on death row."

"Death row?" I whispered.

"Yes."

"Can I think about it and get back to you?"

"Yes. I really think it would be a good thing for you, and I know you will bring a lot to the residents."

"Okay, I promise I'll get back to you in a couple of days."

I drove from the meeting in a slight daze. Death row. How in the world was I qualified to work with men on death row? I'd probably be so scared that I wouldn't be effective. I didn't have the time, and what in the world did I have in common with men on death row?

I chewed on the idea for a few days and asked a few people what they thought. My sponsor thought it was a great idea. Dad thought I'd grown a third eye. With the sweat lodges, other RECs, AA meetings, and the assortment of AA characters I'd befriended, he thought I'd already gone off the deep end. That I was considering walking into death row confirmed it in his eyes.

Don't get me wrong. He appreciated my sobriety and the life it created for me. After all, he'd watched the love of his young life fall head first into alcoholism, destroy our family, cause incalculable pain to his three children, and die of the disease. That was followed by watching helplessly as I fell headfirst into the disease, culminating with his visit as I lay slowly dying on my kitchen floor. My sobriety was as much a miracle to him as it was to me.

But some of the things I did to get and stay sober were way outside of his norm. Every year, I went to his house the day of my AA birthday—more than once smelling of smoke from a sweat lodge—and said, "Well, Pop, I had another sober year."

He always looked at me as if he was thinking, "So did your dog."

When I asked his thoughts about the death row REC, he pushed his long, thin fingers through his thinning red hair and said, "Bring one home for me."

I took that to mean I should do it.

"I'm in," I told Olivia over the phone.

"Perfect. I know this will be an amazing and unique experience for you and will hopefully put some perspective in your life of what is important. We'll meet in a month to start our REC. I need your license and other pertinent information earlier than the other RECs because this is death row. Also, you will be a table leader and give a talk."

She hung up, and all I could think was, *Well, what in the world did I get myself into?*

"Okay, let's gather round and start this first meeting of the Potosi Death Row REC," Olivia announced.

We met at Sally's house. She'd been on the other RECs with me, and I adored her dedication to the REC program. She and most of the outsiders had participated in a death row REC, but a few, like me, were new to working with death row residents. The experienced members were confident and moved through the process in a calm manner while those of us new to working on death row were quiet with our eyes and ears wide open.

Olivia motioned to Sally, and she led us in the *Prayer of Guidance:*

Lord, you promised that when I seek You with all our
heart,
I will find You.
I seek only after You.
Still my troubled heart.
Calm my wayward mind.
I seek only after You.
I'm never going to be able to figure this out on my own,
And right now, I'm leaning heavily on You.
I seek only after You.
I give you all the anxieties and fears I feel inside
I release them all to You
I seek only after You.
I open my life
So that it becomes like an open book before You
May You write in it Your words of inspiration and
direction.
Still my troubled heart.
Calm my wayward mind.
I seek only after You.
I await Your voice.

"Amen."

Olivia then went around the room and handed out talk assignments. Mine was the talk titled *Signs.* There are many signs of God's love and His will if we know where and how to look. Some are those pieces of God that we carry as His inheritance, such as the ability to love and be loved, the effect of joy and laughter on us and its role in our lives, and the order and balance one sees in nature and the universe, to name a few. In my life, I could point to His lifting me from the kitchen floor at my moment of need and then the love that came with my sober path and the joy that came with it all.

There are also signs held within the traditions of faith such as the Eucharist—the taking of bread and wine as communion with Christ—which helps us recognize God's love. There is also baptism, confirmation, confession and penance, marriage, and the last rights. These are God's sacraments that we receive in accordance with and in celebration of Jesus's gifts to the world.

For both, those seen in life and lived through faith, they are signals of God's grace that are perceptible to our intellect and senses.

This talk, *Signs*, is given on the second day, *Rise Day*, and comes before the liturgy—the first act of worship for several of the residents.

When Olivia came to me and simply said, "Signs," my jaw dropped. *You've got to be kidding,* I thought.

"Are you sure you want me to do the talk on signs? I hardly think I'm qualified."

"You are the perfect person."

I looked toward Mary Fran, and she nodded.

I felt like these people didn't have a clue as to who I was, even after all these years. I didn't know a thing about the Eucharist, communion, penance, any of it. Not to mention that by this point, I hadn't done a REC in a couple years.

Why won't she let me do my coming to sobriety talk, I thought, *and be done with it?* I didn't feel like I had a choice but to trust in the process and trust these people, especially Olivia.

I gave a hug to each member of the REC and took my leave, shaking my head all the way out the door.

###

If AA has taught me one thing, it's that there's no shame asking for help. And fortunately, I had help close at hand.

Prior to landing in rehab and then AA, my friend Tom was a Jesuit priest. For one reason or another, sobriety led him away from the priesthood and into the arms of a loving woman. Since it was either be a priest or a husband, not both, he chose to get married and then needed a job. So I hired him. We'd met and become friends in

AA, and my thinking was simple: if he could sell an invisible God, he could sell invisible fences.

"I need to know everything you know about Catholic teachings in a couple weeks," I told him over the phone.

"It's taken me twenty-two years, and a lot of that was school, and I still don't understand it all."

"I just need the best you can offer between selling and installing dog fences in the next month."

"I'll do my best."

I hung up the phone and read the outline for the talk given to me by Olivia. The more I read and thought about it, the more I came to believe the task was way over my head, and I really wasn't sure I could handle it. I started pacing around my house trying to come up with some plausible explanation for Olivia so I could get out of the talk. I came up with a lot of excuses, but plausibility was an issue for each one.

I paused and meditated for a moment, and in that space, I came to the notion that God put this task in front of me for a reason. It must be a sign. The residents need to hear whatever it is I would say, I concluded, but I still wasn't convinced.

I went back to my desk, and on the first page of a five-subject, spiral-bound notebook, I wrote in big letters DEATH ROW REC and beneath that wrote SIGNS. Then I made a list of what I needed to complete the project:

1. *Tom*

2. *Religious books*

3. *Pray, a lot!*

I put my pen down and decided that was good work for day one. Three weeks to go until I presented my talk to the group.

###

The next day, I picked up Tom for work. He walked out of the house smiling and wearing a black robe, surplice, white tunic over the robe, and white clergy collar rather than jeans and a DogWatch shirt. As he approached the truck, he waved the sign of the cross with one hand and in the other was an Aspersorium, a basin of water familiar to all Catholics. I laughed so hard that tears welled in my eyes.

The incident that landed Tom in rehab was when he gave last rights to a dying man in a hospital bed. While sprinkling the man with holy water, he realized to his dismay and the dismay of others in the room that he was sprinkling vodka on the dying patient. He had hidden vodka in an Aspersorium in the church so that other priests wouldn't find it. When he left the church to give the last rights, he grabbed the one filled with vodka.

He was already under close surveillance. He was busted and sent to a rehab for priests in St. Louis. We drunks are quite a group. I often never know whether to laugh or cry.

"That was funny," I said.

He peeled off his priest garb. Underneath were his work clothes. "What can I help you with concerning the Catholic Church?"

"Everything, Tom. I don't know or understand much."

"It's for a talk?"

"Yep. It's on signs, and I'm doing it for a REC on death row."

His expression flattened, and I could tell that the mention of death row woke something inside of him. "Do you have to create it from scratch or do you have a sense of what you might need?"

"I actually have a list." I pulled a small notebook from my shirt pocket. "I need to know the seven signs of the Eucharist, the meaning of communion, the *Paschal Mystery*, the meaning of amen, the meaning of mass, and then the significance of colors in the church."

"Hmm, that's a lot—"

"And I need to know what the *Liturgy of the Word* is, how God and Jesus speak to us, and about a million other things entwined in my personal story."

He let out a slow exhale. "Wow."

"You said it, brother."

For the next couple of weeks, any free time we had during the day, Tom and I talked about the principals and sacraments that underlie the Catholic faith. He was a good teacher, but I could see why he said it took him as long as it did to become fluent in them. To bulk up my preparation, I added a range of books focusing on Catholic theology and relied on the Internet, too. I also reached out to Mary Fran.

When I sat to begin writing, I'd crammed notes into the first three sections of my five-subject notebook. There were even notes running up and down the sides of the pages. Now the easy part. Organize it all, flow my story into it, and create a lively, moving, and profound discussion of the signs of transcendence.

Crickets chirped. The page remained blank.

Okay, okay, Johnny, here we go, I thought and poised above the computer keyboard like a concert pianist about to launch into concerto, and . . . nothing.

One word, just one word . . .

One finger landed on one key, and I had my first word, "I."

WRONG!

"Jesus."

Now we're on to something.

I can't say the words flowed from there, but a week later, I finished writing my talk. The group presentation was a week after that, so I had time to practice.

A few days later, I found myself back in Sally's house, waiting nervously for my turn. When Olivia asked me to deliver what I had written, my throat felt tight, and my hands shook a bit from nerves, but it came out okay. A few members offered constructive criticism, but for the most part, they liked what I'd written.

"Very good, Johnny," Olivia said. "You've come a long way."

"Thank you. I learned a ton. I just hope that whatever comes out of my mouth at Potosi helps the residents." Was I becoming a humbler person?

Mary Fran's eyes perked up. "It will, Johnny, it will."

Then Olivia said, "I picked this topic just for you, Johnny. It is one of the most important talks over the weekend. We believe that of all the outsiders, you are the one person who can relate to the residents more than anyone else. You'll be close to most of their ages, ninety-five-percent are incarcerated due in part to drugs and alcohol, and you are male. Not many of them are going to listen to a talk on signs coming from a woman.

"Get some rest over the next couple of weeks. This is going to be stressful and extremely wearing. Try to eat well, ask friends and family for Palanca letters, and ask for prayers while praying for yourself. There is a tremendous difference between a REC on death row and one at a maximum or minimum correctional facility."

If I wasn't nervous before, I was now.

As soon as I got into my car: *God, grant me the serenity to accept the things I cannot change, courage to change the things I can, and the wisdom to know the difference.*

A few hundred of those, and I left.

CHAPTER 9
THAT BIT OF
GOD WITHIN US

POTOSI IS ABOUT an hour southwest of St. Louis. Not really considered the Ozarks, it's still out in the hills and away from any densely populated areas.

The daffodils and tulips had come and gone, and the countryside was starting to show signs of a gorgeous spring. Redbuds—small trees with pinkish-red flowers—were in bloom and dotted the gently greening hillsides. The trees had not yet budded, and I could see through them into the sun-speckled woods.

As with my first REC, the tunes were loud, the top was down, and the weather was filled with promise and renewal. I felt prepared for what I would encounter. In the two weeks leading up to the REC, I increased my weekly AA meetings, got plenty of rest, ate a high-protein diet, exercised, prayed on my knees at least twice a day, and said the serenity prayer more times than I could count.

Before joining the team at our motel, I drove out toward the prison so that my first look at it wasn't as we were being led in by the guards. After a few miles, the sprawling compound came into view. It was enormous with barbed wire, low-to-the-ground gray buildings, and a guard tower jutting up out of the middle of the prison. Like the eye of Sauron in *The Lord of the Rings*, it could see all below and around it.

Greening spring grass flowed up to the barbed wire, but behind the wire, the entirety of it was gray, metallic, and looked like the deep, colorless cold of winter. My heart beat a little faster, my palms were sweaty, and I felt overwhelmed and over my head. The prison was frightening, and all I could think was, *Who am I to tell these men there are signs of God all around them?* From all appearances, they lived under very difficult circumstances.

The motel was a simple affair like any motel one would find at most of the exits off Interstate 70, which stretches from Pittsburgh to Fishlake National Forest in Utah. I chuckled a little at the thought that we'd found the perfect middle ground between the Ritz and Potosi prison.

Most of the members were already there and waved as I pulled in. Rather than tunes blaring and the look of a man on vacation, my entrance was humbler, lower key, but happy to see these friends. We'd become a family over the past RECs, and we knew we could count on each other to give our best.

We loaded the vans with food, soda, Bibles, banners, hymnals, and the rest of the paraphernalia we would need for *Die Day* and what we could leave overnight. Though we all were staying at the hotel, we didn't check in. Instead, we climbed in the vans and pulled out of the motel parking lot. Behind us, dark clouds loomed, and thunderstorms were in the forecast. Outside the front window, it was a blue-sky day in the direction of the prison.

Our first stop wasn't the front gate of the prison. Instead, it was Waffle House. This was our tradition and a good one since it gave us one last chance to fill up on delicious, greasy food before the ordeal of a prison cafeteria.

As we waited for our food, Olivia and Mary Fran reminded us of some of the details. There would be sixteen outsiders and sixty residents, which was a slightly smaller ratio than on some past RECs. This would allow a bit more personal interaction with each resident. There would be eight tables with seven residents at each, and four would help in the kitchen. Once again, I was a table leader and at a table without any other outsiders.

We ate our fill of golden waffles and crispy bacon and drank tons of coffee then paid up and left to arrive at the prison by 9 a.m.

The storm hadn't reached us yet, but the branches of the few trees near the prison were bouncing in the wind. The redbuds in the distance waved like Chinese ribbon dancers. Dandelions poked their yellow heads up through early green grass, and azalea bushes showed off their bright colors. I loved springtime in Missouri. The air was fragrant with the scents of grass, trees, and flowers.

Behind us, the storm started to catch up. As beautiful as spring is, it can also include dangerous storms that sometimes whirl into tornadoes. This was one of those storms, and meteorologists had issued warnings for that morning.

I wasn't sure if my fellow outsiders were quiet because of the impending storm or the impending entry onto death row, but we rode in silence. Tony, the music director, drove the van I was in and softly started to hum "Amazing Grace." After a few bars, we all chimed in and started singing. The power of the beautiful song carried us through the main gate and up to the entrance.

We parked so that the prison consumed the entire windscreen with its imposing mass. My stomach ached, and my throat tightened. All signs of a REC.

Olivia and Mary Fran walked up into the lobby to check in but came back out soon after.

"They're threatening to shut down the REC for the weekend," Olivia said. "The warden said there was a fight in the yard and to check back in an hour. Let's pray."

We all said the serenity prayer, which seemed appropriate given our powerlessness to change the course of the day. Then we got out of the vans and some of us smoked and we all made small talk. The storm was approaching quickly, and we could see lightening followed a few seconds later by rumbling thunder.

Olivia went back to check with the warden. The storm was almost on top of us, and I could feel electricity in the air. Lightning hit closer, and loud claps of thunder broke over our heads as we flew back into the vans. Rain followed by hail fell in loud rasps against the roof of the van, and tornado alarms wailed all around us. The sky turned an aqua green, and the wind howled and rocked the van with the force of each gust. We looked out the window for signs of a funnel beginning to form.

"Look," Tony said.

We turned toward the entrance of the prison, and there was Olivia, leaning out the door and waving us in.

"Hallelujah," some of us yelled, but we still had to stay in the vans for another twenty minutes to let the worst of the storm pass.

Before long, the wind and rain eased, and the tornado alarms went silent. If the guards inside were intent on demonstrating they were in charge, God showed who was really in charge. I suppose I shouldn't have been too surprised that with the passing of the storm, my jangling nerves passed as well.

We joined hands and shouted, "For the residents!"

Olivia walked to the vans and explained that the residents broke the fight up and the warden had given us his blessing and wished us a good REC. We grabbed the supplies and, arms full, we entered a sterile, nondescript entryway. Multiple cameras watched us from above, and the guards' faces were set in angry-looking grimaces.

One by one we lined up, and a guard photographed each of us. A female guard told the women to be sure they buttoned their shirts to the neck and not to let the male residents touch them inappropriately.

"For your own security," the female guard said, "do not, and I repeat, do not give your last name, address, or phone number to any prisoner. If for some reason one of the men reaches parole and is released, you do not want him looking you up. These men are the worst of the worst. Please keep that in mind."

She gave a stern look to all of us.

"I will be taking you through a series of locked gates and finally through an airlock holding area that only supports four of you at a time to run cameras, metal detectors, and other identifying devices over you. This is for your protection."

There was not a word spoken for the next fifteen minutes.

What in the world am I doing in this place? I thought.

We passed through a metal detector and then a gated door opened automatically in front of us. We walked down a hallway and heard the door slam and lock behind us. With that, another large door opened in front of us. I looked at my fellow REC members, and there were only nervous smiles. It was as if we were entering a perverse Willy Wonka factory.

We walked through the door to our front, and after the last of us passed through, it slammed shut and locked.

"Okay," said the female guard, "four at a time into the holding area. The airlocks will open on this side until you are all in safely and will close and lock behind you. It will only take a few minutes for the all-clear."

A loud swoosh came from the airlock, and the door in front of us opened. I was in the third group. We stated our names, addresses, and Social Security numbers. There was a thick pane of glass on one wall of the airlock, and we could see guards running security checks as if we were in some sort of futuristic movie. Once satisfied, they gave the all-clear, and there was a whooshing sound as the airlocks on the next door released and opened the door.

Rather than enter some fantastical mystery world, I walked through that door into the prison yard where I stood with my fellow REC members waiting for the last of our group.

There was no way to miss that this was a different game. There were many residents in the yard, and they started to walk in our direction. I noticed that the tattoos on these men were different from those on the residents of past RECS at Farmington and Vandalia, and they were more prevalent. Some had a teardrop design falling out of the corner of one eye. Some were just the outline, and some were filled in with ink. Those that were just an outline signaled the loss of a friend. The solid tattoos signaled the friend's life was avenged.

Spiderweb tattoos on elbows signified they were entrapped, and clocks with no hands denoted long-term residents. I saw dots on their hands or under their eyes that meant *My crazy life*, and a few had *ACAB*, which either meant *All cops are bad* or, as I hoped, *Always carry a Bible.*

Other than these tattoos, there were crosses, pictures of scantily clad women, initials, and just about anything else a person could imagine. And they were on every patch of visible skin.

A few of the residents called out, "Jesus freaks," "Holy rollers," and "Come here, little girl . . . where is your God now?" Of course, interspersed between each word was a series of obscenities.

"BACK OFF!" yelled a guard.

"You coming to save us?" yelled a shaved-head resident.

I was ready to run. It was crazy.

"SINGLE FILE! LET'S GO!" yelled a guard.

We marched through the yard and toward a gray building that I assumed would be our sanctuary. I couldn't wait to get there.

Another gate and lock opened, and we double-timed it into the building.

I turned to Barbara, a veteran of death row RECs, and said, "Wow!"

She didn't need to say anything. I could tell by her look that I needed to calm down, that everything was fine.

The guards in the building checked our photo IDs one more time. It seemed excessive to me, but then I remembered, *Shut up, Lipscomb. You should've checked your ego in at the first door. These guys are in charge here, not you.*

Olivia stepped to the center of our sanctuary. "All right, guys, you know the drill."

Like the well-coordinated worker bees we were, we set about turning our fifty-foot-by-fifty-foot room into a place of calm and faith. It seemed a little ironic that we were holding *Die Day* on death row. I'd asked Olivia earlier how many of the residents were on death row. She said about a third. The rest were in for long sentences and many without the possibility of parole. Most of their convictions were for murder and rape. I didn't ask then or at any time during the REC, but I'm sure the stories of their crimes were ugly.

"Oh, okay. No problem," I lied.

I also knew that alcohol and drugs were in one way or another part of their stories. Who was I to judge? Any one of the hundreds, maybe even thousands, of nights I drove intoxicated, I could have killed somebody. It wouldn't have been intentional, but what was the difference? I would have taken a life. I also knew that in each of my many, many blackouts, I was beyond my own mind's rationality. Violence is not inherently part of my makeup, but I've heard enough peaceful people tell stories of violence and abuse to know that alcohol can open a door that for sober people remains firmly closed.

The sanctuary set a somber tone with the darker colors used on the *Die Day* banners. Tony played slower, mournful gospel songs on his guitar, and there was little if any talking or joking around.

Maybe it was just my apprehension, but there was a different feel to this REC. Even the normally chatty Sally was tempered, and Olivia didn't bark orders.

Mary Fran called us together for a prayer.

> *Jesus, I will arise; Jesus do thou accompany me;*
> *Jesus, do thou lock my heart into thine,*
> *And let my body and my soul*
> *Be commended unto thee.*
> *The Lord is crucified.*
> *May God guard and protect my senses*
> *So that misfortunes may not overcome me.*
> *In the name of God, the Father, Son, and the Holy Ghost.*
> *Amen!*

A collective amen responded to her.

Four guards approached us, and Harry, a muscular, slightly overweight man told us the rules one more time and assured us we were safe. "Just follow our direction," he emphasized.

"STAY IN LINE OR WE WILL CANCEL THIS REC!" came a loud voice from outside our sanctuary.

I heard the humming of indistinct voices, all trying to speak at the same time.

"MOVE OUT!"

I heard footsteps approaching the sanctuary, and an electric bolt of fear ran up my spine. We lined up to meet the residents, and I faded to the back of the line, wanting at least a moment or two to size these men up before greeting them.

"GET BACK FROM THE DOORWAY!" Harry barked.

We all stepped five paces back.

I half expected the door to swing open to a snarling beast restrained by dozens of chains and handlers.

Tony started to play "Amazing Grace" on his guitar, and we started to sing.

The sound of soft-soled shoes came closer then stopped. The door opened, and the first resident passed through, and then the remainder poured in.

Smiles abounded. *What the heck . . .* I thought. These guys were happy, really happy to see us. High fives were given and received. Those who knew Olivia, Mary Fran, and Sally from previous RECs and programs hugged them. Almost all the men entered singing and taking dance-like steps. The only time I remembered a group of residents walking into *Die Day* with this level of joy and openness was the women at Vandalia.

My simple brain had a hard time rationalizing what I was seeing. These men had committed horrible crimes, were locked up for life or facing execution, and they were happy, dancing, and singing. *What in the world is going on?*

Later, I asked Olivia how they could be so happy with what they face each day, the haunting memories of their crimes, and looming state-sanctioned death.

"You will find, Johnny, that these men will be extremely open from the beginning, and they will let you in, much like the women at Vandalia. The odds of them getting back into the world are slim, so they have let go and let God into their lives. They will trust you, they won't have big egos, and they will tell you anything you want to know.

"You see, the men in Farmington will be getting out someday, so they have to keep up their tough appearances. Because of that, it takes them a while to let their walls down and let God in.

"Do you understand?"

"I guess."

These men had tattoos all over, were muscular, and each one carried his personal Bible with numerous page markers and worn covers. These Bibles did not sit idly on a shelf.

And their smiles were infectious. The whole room, except for the guards, sang "Amazing Grace" and swayed to the rhythm and melody.

Olivia stepped to the center of the room. "Okay, okay, find your name at a table and have a seat."

I was at table six with Juan, Van, Leroy, Jasper, Bob, Manuel, Robert, and John. I introduced myself and then asked each man to do the same. When I came to Jasper, I was in awe. He was at least six feet eight inches tall and two hundred eighty pounds (probably more given the mass of muscles on him). He reminded me of the actor, Michael Clark Duncan, who played John Coffey, the prisoner on death row in the movie *The Green Mile*.

I reached my hand out to shake Jasper's, and when he closed his hand around mine, it disappeared within his. He smiled and said, "Hi, John. Welcome to Potosi." His voice was deep and calm.

"I'm happy to make your acquaintance, too, Jasper."

In his large, clear eyes, I saw sadness, compassion, regret, kindness, and the enduring weariness of a hard life that only comes from those who have seen and lived the worst and come back. Jasper was different.

"What should we call our table?" I asked. "And not the Bloods or the Crips or anything like that."

It was a risky joke to make, but I got a chuckle out of them. We bantered around a few names and concurred with *The Eight Disciples of Jesus*.

So little old me and the eight disciples were ready to take on the weekend at table six.

###

Olivia stood at the center of the room. "Okay, guys. Now that we've met our tablemates, let's start focusing on the importance of the weekend and today, which if you know or don't know is themed *Die Day.*"

Mary Fran took over at this point. "Unless the grain of wheat falls to the ground and dies, it remains but a seed. This day is all about change. God, our father, has always been there for us. We left him—he didn't leave us. We need rebirth and recommitment of our spiritual life and a reconciliation and celebration of our Father's loving forgiveness."

From there, we performed the *Bible Enthronement* and the day's reading from John 12:24 and Romans 6:4. John discusses the transformation from a single seed to many, and Romans states that just as Christ was raised from the dead through the glory of the Father, we too may live a new life when reborn with faith.

With the announcement of the readings, the residents opened their Bibles and turned without a word to the correct page and reading. It took about two seconds. Looking around my table, I could see they had highlighted the readings, underlined them, or put a Post-It note to mark the location in their books. Bob, one of my tablemates, helped me find the readings much faster than I would have on my own.

Then, as if in a single voice, we read aloud.

"Amen," "Praise Jesus," and "Hallelujah" echoed through our sanctuary.

Tony leaped in and called us to sing "At the Cross."

> *There's a place where mercy reigns and never dies,*
> *There's a place where streams of grace flow deep and*
> *wide . . .*

The residents seemed to know the song by heart, and I could tell that in their minds, they'd left prison and death row for at least a moment. They were in church and in the presence of God, which lifted their troubles from them.

They were living in the present, in the now rather than consumed by the past and what was to come for them. In AA, this is an important but challenging thing to do. The idea is that I will not worry or allow my past to consume me, nor will I allow my concerns for the future to become wounds. I am happy to not be drinking in this moment, and I will build my sobriety one moment at a time until it becomes a natural flow of sober, mindful moments.

It is a form of meditation and one that can take years or even a lifetime to achieve. And yet, these men were in that state in what appeared to be the speed of a single thought. It's not that they didn't harbor regrets, but for the time being, they weren't concerned about the past, and the future didn't own territory in their consciousness. They were purely in the moment and stood before God.

After the hymn, Sally stepped to the front of the sanctuary and gave the *Ideals and Christian Maturity* talk. This led to table discussions of the ideals of youth and adulthood, how God fit into their young and adult lives, and what they were doing today and in the future to fulfill God's will.

At my table, I was more of a traffic cop than leader as these men wanted to discuss their thoughts and experiences in one breath. At Farmington, it took a day and a half for the men to reach this level of openness. These men seemed even more immediately open than the women at Vandalia.

Afterward, we sang a hymn, and the Wheaties brought out a snack of vegetables, fruit, and juice.

"COUNT!" called a guard.

The residents leaped up and counted off in quick succession then, when cleared, came back to their tables. It was one of the most efficient activities I've ever witnessed. At its heart, I believe, was the true desire of these men to limit the duration and impact of these intrusions on their time with the Lord.

Mary Fran gave the *Death and Resurrection* talk, which discusses the *Paschal Mystery* (the death and resurrection of Christ). She stressed that this weekend was about choice and the opportunity for change. Will we accept God's love for us, will we accept his life for us, let go of the past, give our hurts and pains to the Lord, begin a new life, and share ourselves with Jesus?

She talked about how suffering brings about growth, growth means a change in attitude, growth means struggle, and we will fall short, we will hurt others, but we can forgive, and we will hurt ourselves, but God will heal us.

She continued speaking about how the weekend will give us the opportunity to grow with Christ, die to ourselves, embrace our pain, rise to a new life with Jesus, and go forth and share ourselves with Jesus and others.

"How will we grow?" she asked us. "We will relax, forget about the past and future, and live with Jesus in the moment. Let yourself be open to new possibilities and opportunities and take a risk, meet Christ!"

"Praise Jesus, God bless," rose from our many voices.

As Mary Fran finished, Tony played "Swing Low Sweet Chariot." As those first oh-so-familiar lyrics came from my voice, I recognized that without having intentionally learned the lyrics to this and other hymns, I knew these songs. It wasn't through my private school education nor was it from church—I hadn't been in church long enough—but I knew these songs.

Then a thought came to me, and warmth rose from my gut along with an image of Lizzy, the woman who raised me when Mom couldn't or wouldn't. She hummed and sang these songs as she worked in the kitchen or sat to rest. Often, she'd look at me and say, "John David, sing with me."

"Yes, ma'am."

In our sanctuary, the lyrics flowed like molasses as some deep emotional connection moved each person's voice. Whether it was of their present circumstances or a haunting memory from their past, we all felt the power of this song and the shared experience of singing it. Tears welled in my eyes as I felt anew the beauty of these moments with Lizzy and what her loss meant to me. Jasper, like some big, loving bear, laid a hand on my shoulder as we sang.

I was supposed to be there for him, not the other way around. When I turned to look up at him, pain that I could not imagine reddened his eyes. I felt safe, in good company. I forgot about my past and my many flaws and indiscretions and for that moment lived in the presence of God and Jesus. I was no saint, and there were people I'd hurt—most painfully, my children—but God unshackled me from the things that haunted me. It was not forever but in His presence. Atonement is a lifelong practice.

"LINE UP! LUNCH TIME!" Harry the guard shouted.

After a lunch of sardines, potato chips, bread, salad, and Jell-O, we could sit out in the yard and have a smoke. We told jokes and laughed, talked about favorite sports teams—most were St. Louis Cardinals fans—and connected in a less formal way.

It was clear they could watch sports. "What else do you do?" I asked.

"We obviously can't do everything you, being a free person, can do," Jasper said. "Our family and friends don't come to visit. Many of us have a good part of our family in here with us. Even though the food is a misery, we get three square meals a day, time to visit our friends, watch TV, go to church services, and so on, but all in all, it's still boring and degrading. The guards don't allow any slack, and they stick to a very tight schedule. Make no doubt about it, we know who's in charge and what happens if we get out of line."

"The hole," a few said.

"I've heard of the hole. What is it?"

"Solitary confinement. There used to be an actual hole, but now it's just a windowless room with no other residents."

"How do you end up there?"

"Many ways, my man. Fighting, trying to escape, giving a hard time to the *kitty-kitties.*"

"The what?"

"The women guards."

"Oh."

"We have plenty of time to read, and most of us at this REC get together for Bible study."

"LET'S GO, LADIES!" Harry yelled.

"We have a lot to cover this afternoon and evening," Olivia said to the room. "Van from table six is now going to give the talk on *The Prodigal Son.*"

"My man, Van," I said as I clapped for him. He emerged from the kitchen where the Wheaties had prayed over him, and he walked to the front of the room with a big, nervous smile. "Break a leg, Van."

He started to speak, and at first nerves stilted his words, but as he continued, he gained his footing and through his story described that God would forgive us, no matter what we've done, if we turn to Him and ask for his love and forgiveness. It is the ultimate and should be the easiest of amends that we ask for, but for so many, myself included, it can be the hardest.

The Prodigal Son also hit close to home for me. Found in Luke 15:11-32, it tells the story of a son who asks for and receives his inheritance from his father but then squanders it on wild living in a far-off land. Destitute, the son returns to the father to beg his forgiveness and ask that his father take him in as a servant. Instead, the father rejoices and calls for a celebration of his son's return. "He was lost and is found," reads the text.

The brother sees the celebration and out of jealousy complains that while he was near his father and lived a good life, there was never a celebration of his goodness. The father repeats to him, "My son, you are always with me, and everything I have is yours, but we had to celebrate and be glad, because this brother of yours was dead and is alive again. He was lost and is found."

I had been the prodigal son who was dead to my father but now was found, and his love for me remained. Though I am thankful for both Dad's love and forgiveness as well as God's love and forgiveness, I do wonder about the other son. When I look at the other outsiders, I see the other sons. People who to my knowledge have lived good lives. Perhaps none is free of sin, but to what reward is their goodness?

It seems to be an easier, richer life lived within His grace and love, but while that is well and good, I still wonder about it. Are we all sinners and therefore all prodigal sons who at one point or another need to return and ask forgiveness of God, the Father? I looked around the room at the insiders, knowing that some were slated for death. I couldn't help but think of a line from many movies where the avenger or murderer says something like, "You may be forgiven in the next world, but not in this one and not by me."

If we follow the example of Jesus and ask what He would do, are we not bound to live by His creed?

Metanoia was the next talk. It also discusses the concept of forgiveness and acceptance but focuses on repentance, specifically the individual's ability and duty to repent. By asking for forgiveness and then repentance, we can undergo a transformative change of heart.

Joan gave this talk, and once again I found myself in deep thought.

Repent means to feel and express regret for a trespass against another or God. I could go on and on about my own sins against those whom I should have loved. The list is long, and at its very top are my children. I still feel guilt for these things I've done. After all, I am accountable for my actions.

I dug a little deeper into this and recognized that repentance can also be expressed to mean that one dies by turning away from sin and then is reborn through amendment of one's life. Step Nine of the twelve steps in AA compels a person to make direct amends to those we've hurt. I have actively done this, but I have also done what I could to make living amends. Staying sober is not enough. I must also strive to be a good person and help others.

I looked at my tablemates. I have seen in their openness and kindness that they are working, despite their imperfections and pasts, to make living amends. Prison is in and of itself a forced amend and repentance, but the efforts of these men led me to understand in a deeper way that hadn't penetrated in the other RECs that God is here.

My eyes were opening in ways they never had before to His signs. He is always communicating to us, if only we'd pull the cotton from our ears and the blinders from our eyes.

Tony strummed a few chords on his guitar and called out, "Let's sing 'Awesome God.'" Then he led us in with, "When He rolls up his sleeves, he ain't just putting on the Ritz . . ."

The residents joined in without a moment's hesitation. They clapped, smiled, and laughed as they sang at the top of their lungs. It was yet another moment of pure happiness that no new car or home or vacation could ever help anyone achieve. Together, we outsiders and insiders were coming together to create this moment.

"Hey, hey, hey!" a man and then another called out. Silence, and in that I heard a struggle and turned to see two men fighting, each trying to wrestle the other while landing blows. Despite the warnings and training, I didn't know what to do.

I didn't know what to do, but the residents acted as if they'd rehearsed for this moment. A group of them put themselves in front of the gated door so that the guards couldn't see what was going on as another group grabbed the two residents and pulled them off each other. They then sat them down away from each other and gave them a quick talk.

Within thirty seconds, a potentially explosive, REC-canceling situation was over, and everyone was back in their chairs.

"What was that all about?" I asked Jasper.

"Don't know and don't care as long as it was under control before anyone was the wiser." He gave me a wink, and I dropped the subject.

In the next instant, the Wheaties appeared with cookies and soda. A welcome distraction. Who knew that fresh-baked cookies could bring peace?

With calm restored, there was another talk that focused on the notion of forgiveness and the ability of a person to be reborn through the sacrament of *Reconciliation*. In other words, making peace with God. Afterward, the residents could enter a makeshift confessional and confess their sins with a priest the REC directors had appointed during preparation for the REC. For many, it was the first time they had gone through confession. The priest kept in strictest confidence what they said and confessed, but the power of the experience was written on each man's face as he emerged from the confessional.

This was the hardest and most important part of *Die Day*. For some, it was life-changing because it marked a point where these men were willing to change and wanted to accept God into their lives and live by His word—from a thug into a Christian brother helping and looking out for others.

As the last man exited the confessional, Harry called out, "LINE UP! DINNERTIME!"

As we approached the dining hall, a familiar odor assaulted my olfactory senses. At the entrance, the menu board read: Chicken

Chow Mein, Chicken Gravy, Green Beans, Rice, Pease & Carrots, Bread, Margarine, and Apple.

Jasper picked up a tray, and I said, "Lots of ketchup and salt, right, my big friend?"

He gave me a hard, withering glare. "This is one of the better meals, and I can't wait."

Note to self, I thought, *keep your big, stupid mouth shut.*

When we sat down, I noticed that most of the residents enjoyed the meal. I guessed that the food here was all they were going to get, so over weeks, months, and years, they adjusted to where they looked forward to meals. The more I looked around with my newly opened eyes, I saw that this was time they could spend with friends they couldn't see on their cellblock. Some of them even sat down as families. It was a huge change from the maximum and minimum-security RECs where the residents loathed the food.

I held my nose and choked down the chow mein. I swear some of the noodles moved.

After dinner, Mary Fran described the *Service of Ashes*, which is the ritual act of dying to then be reborn the following day.

"Quietly, think about an incident in your life that's troubling you and for which you would like forgiveness or healing. Write it down on a piece of paper."

We did this, and then a server collected the pieces of paper in an urn and brought it to our altar. Mary Fran then led us in a prayer:

Almighty and merciful God,
You have brought us together in the name of your Son to
receive mercy and grace in our time of need.
Open our eyes to see the evil we have done.
Touch our hearts and turn us to you.
Where sin has divided and scattered,
may your power heal and strengthen;

where sin has brought death,
may your Spirit raise to new life.
Give us a new heart to love you
so that our lives may reflect the image of your Son.
May the world see the glory of Christ
revealed in your Church and come to know
that He is the one whom you have sent,
Jesus Christ, your Son, our Lord and brother.

The papers were burned, and one by one we approached the altar where the community priest put a cross from the ashes on each forehead. With that, he said, "Turn away from sin and follow the Gospel."

Mary Fran stood at the center of the room, and with a look of sincerity and respect, she said, "Dear friends, through the *Paschal Mystery* we have been buried with Christ in baptism so that we may rise with him to a new life. Now that we have admitted our sinfulness and turned back to the Lord, let us renew the promises we made in baptism when we rejected Satan and his works and promised to serve God faithfully in his holy Catholic Church.

"Do you reject Satan?"

"Yes!" replied the room.

"And all his works?"

"Yes!"

"And all his empty promises?"

"Yes!"

"Do you believe in God the Father Almighty, creator of heaven and earth?"

"I do!"

"Do you believe in Jesus Christ, His only son, our Lord, who was born of the Virgin Mary, was crucified, died, and was buried, rose from death, and is now seated at the right hand of the Father?"

"I do!"

"Do you believe in the Holy Spirit, the Holy Catholic Church, the Communion of Saints, the forgiveness of sins, the resurrection of the body, and life everlasting?"

"I do!"

"This is our faith. This is the faith of the Church. We are proud to profess it in Christ Jesus the Lord. God, the all-powerful Father of our Lord Jesus Christ, has given us a new birth by water and the Holy Spirit and has forgiven our sins. May He also keep us faithful to our Lord Jesus Christ forever and ever. Amen."

"AMEN!"

The room had worked itself into a frenzy. The guards seemed nervous, but the men were high on Jesus and God, and so was I. We were ready to march to the Pearly Gates professing our love for Jesus. There was clapping and dancing, and there were abundant smiles and chants of "praise Jesus" and "amen." We were saved.

Olivia rose. "Okay, okay, let's settle down please." She paused and waited for all eyes to be on her. "It is now 9:45 p.m., and hundreds of people are sending their prayers to you. Now that you have died to yourselves, you are now alive with Christ in a community of believers, both inside and outside of this correctional facility."

"Tomorrow is *Rise Day*. Get some rest. It will be a long day!"

"LINE UP!" Harry yelled.

The men left singing "Amazing Grace," its beautiful lament and plea trailing down the hallway after them. We cleaned up our sanctuary and prepped it for the next day then exited through the series of airlocks, gates, and doors back out into a pitch-black early spring evening.

At the hotel, Olivia came to me. "You're up tomorrow, Johnny. It's an important talk, and I know you can handle it. Get some sleep." She started to walk away but then turned. "Thank you for your service."

"Thank you, too."

I sat out in the cool air thinking of Jasper and the Eight Disciples of Jesus.

CHAPTER 10
THE SADDEST STORY
I EVER HEARD

A DAY THAT CHANGES your life, for good or bad, starts like any other.

Or maybe not.

The last airlock swooshed, and the large, impossibly heavy-looking door opened to the prison yard where the last four of us met the members of our team. All eyes were on us, and a few called out taunts and insults. A few walked toward us, but they did not come close enough to raise the ire of the guards.

In the sanctuary, we hung banners for *Rise Day* while the Wheaties prepared cookies and fresh fruit for the residents. Cans of soda were placed on each table. Balloons and streamers hung from the walls and were strung across the ceiling (as best we could). Death row looked colorful and festive.

Outside the door, down the hallway, we heard the persistent clap of rubber-soled shoes on cement and the hum of sixty voices.

"STAY IN LINE!" I recognized Harry's voice. "GET BACK FROM THE DOORWAY!"

In unison, we shuffled back a few steps.

Jeremiah was a bullfrog . . . rang out at full blast and echoed in the room. The door opened, and residents entered the room like football players breaking through a paper banner into a crowded stadium. We outsiders were lined up on either side of them, and we greeted each other with smiles, laughter, high fives, dancing, and singing. I had to stand on the tips of my toes to give Jasper a high five.

We danced to "Jeremiah" and then to "My God is an Awesome God." In the midst of it all, I realized that these men, the lifers and those with death sentences waiting for their appeals to save them or be exhausted, may never have another opportunity to feel so free among friends—unless they could find joy in AA and/or church.

Olivia raised her arms. "Okay, all right everybody, let's settle down. We have a lot to cover today. How is everybody?"

Huge applause. "God bless. Thank you, Olivia. Praise Jesus."

Things quieted, and the men found their way to their tables and set upon the fruit, cookies, and soda.

Jasper sat his large body next to me. "How are you today, John?"

"Awesome, really awesome. You guys ready for today?"

"Yes, sir.

"If it dies," exclaimed Mary Fran, "it produces much fruit. We see Jesus as our brother, and his life of service, sacrifice, and attending to the needs of others is an example of how to be a true Christian. On this second day, *Rise Day*, we foster a growth of our relationship with Jesus the Son. Jesus's resurrection and our resurrection from our life of sin brings about new life and opportunities. Take this day and embrace it.

"Praise Jesus, for He has arisen. Hallelujah!"

"Hallelujah!"

I was in the moment and felt true, God-given joy that can only be gained through helping others. We are all equal in the eyes of

God and Jesus when we atone, and no truer words could be spoken of my life and this moment than *But for the grace of God go I . . .*

"PRAISE JESUS!" Jasper called out in his deep bass voice that startled me.

Mary Fran began the *Bible Enthronement* and discussed the meaning of *Rise Day* a bit more. Tony rose from his spot by his guitar and boom box, but before he could speak —

"COUNT!"

Like a well-practiced team, the residents stood in line and counted off then returned to their seats.

They were so quick that Tony barely had a chance to recompose himself before all eyes were upon him. "Anybody up for '10,000 Reasons'?"

And we began, *Bless the Lord oh my soul . . .*

As the lyrics tumbled from my mouth, a nagging little thought blossomed. *Am I a fraud?* I didn't think this because I doubted my faith or conviction, but because I wondered if I was the right messenger to speak to these men, men facing life behind bars and death, on the signs of God's love. When I saw Mary Fran stand before these people and Olivia guide and direct each day as well as the talks given by the others, it was hard for me to feel as if I was their equal. In fact, I believed — and still believe — that I was not.

My story and what I have to give, I thought, *is not nearly enough.* And that made me think that to these residents and perhaps even to the others of the team of outsiders, I would appear to be more of a death row tourist rather than God and Jesus's docent.

Olivia said I was the perfect person to give this important talk, but who was I to think I could render anything to these men? Was I just another dime-a-dozen drunk? I knew this weekend and this day was not about me, but I hardly felt I was enough. So far, I felt more like a passenger than guide, student more than teacher.

###

Dorothy gave the first talk of the day on *People of God as Community of Love*. It was a discussion of the concept of community and that being a member of an active and thriving community requires each person to make use of their gifts and talents for the common good. A simple enough idea, but when she said, "We suffer with each other, and we celebrate life with each other," I was caught off guard by the simple beauty and truth of that sentiment.

At our table, we tossed around what it means to be in a community and that with God, Jesus, and church, we are entering a community where we support each other and our faith, and are in return supported.

"LINE UP! LUNCH!" Harry called out.

"I can't wait," I said under my breath. I turned to Manuel and asked, "What's on the menu for today?"

"Chicken patty, gravy, potatoes, and bread."

I'd gotten better about not expressing my disgust, but my stomach hadn't. I sat with the Eight Disciples of Jesus, and we laughed, joked around, and debated whether the Cardinals had a chance this baseball season. By now, I'd learned that to avoid humiliating myself, I needed to keep quiet about the food and not assume I knew more about Bible verses than The Disciples. I could say the first two words of a verse and these guys would already have their Bibles open to the exact page and finish the sentence and discuss its meaning.

During lunch, I learned I didn't know diddly about sports—especially basketball and baseball—compared to these guys. *It must have been between seasons when these guys committed their crimes*, I joked to myself.

At our smoke break, Jasper asked, "John, I hear you're giving a talk?"

"I am, and I can't begin to tell you how nervous I am."

"You're among friends, man. Picture us in our underwear, as the experts say."

I laughed, and so did the others, but my self-doubt continued to nag at me.

Tom, one of the outsiders, gave the *Christian Life* talk and as with Dorothy's, I took so much from it. Then in our table discussion, I was more of a traffic cop to the competing voices wanting to express their thoughts. As with each talk and discussion, I felt that I was receiving so much wisdom, joy, and growth in my understanding of faith, but giving back so little in return.

Later, the Wheaties brought out cookies and coffee as well as Palanca letters. The letter addressed to me was from one of the team of outsiders and read:

> *Dear Team Member,*
>
> *Today is* Rise Day*! Another day filled and graced by Jesus! The song in my heart for you this day is from* Be Not Afraid. *Be not afraid, I go before you always, come, follow me, and I will give you rest. Continue to know that Jesus loves you so very much.*
>
> *Your friend in Jesus,*
>
> *Janet*

Just what I needed. How did she know?

Olivia rose. "We are going to start our Chapel visits in just a minute. We will go table by table, and those tables not involved in the visit, please pray among yourselves. If you do not know, your table leader will teach you how to pray the rosary, pray the Stations of the Cross, and explain in more detail the mass. Please try to remain as quiet as possible for those in the chapel."

A mock chapel was set off the kitchen area, and table one was first to enter.

I looked at the Eight Disciples. "Are you guys able to pray to the Stations of the Cross? There're fourteen."

"We know how," Manuel said.

Duh, Johnny. "No, sorry, I meant is there a chapel here?"

"No," said Jasper.

Double duh, Johnny.

"But what I do," Jasper continued, "is I start facing our altar and turn fourteen times praying to each station." He paused. "I do look forward to getting out and praying properly at regular church stations."

I couldn't touch what he'd just said, so I changed the subject. "Do you know how to pray to the Rosary?"

"Yes," they all affirmed.

Mary Fran called out, "Table six, your turn."

We went to the small DIY chapel and sat in a circle with a crucifix. This was our chance to speak in an impromptu and personal way with God and Jesus. I've had some yell, others cry, and many more speak to Jesus as if he were sitting in front of us, listening with his legs crossed.

The crucifix was in my hand, so I went first. "I've sinned against you many times in the past, but I am now your servant. Thank you for this new life and the ability to continue Your work." I handed the crucifix to Leroy.

He had been quiet, and this was no different. He mouthed some words, a few of us leaned closer to hear, and then he passed the crucifix to the next man.

Bob was mad. "Why have you left me here?" he growled. He claimed he was wrongly accused and that despite his innocence he had still been still convicted and imprisoned. He yelled at God and Jesus for abandoning him to this fate and cried that he'd worked so hard to live a life free of sin and atonement, and yet he was left in this dark and horrible place.

It was not my job to interfere, and especially not to give anyone false hope, so I did my best to listen and have compassion for a man so obviously in pain. When he finished, I said, "Welcome home, brother. All answers are here."

He didn't buy it and gave me a glare.

Jasper, John, and Manuel paid their respects to Jesus and God. I could tell this helped them get some of the burden they carried off their shoulders. At the same time, hearing their pain made me wonder more intensely why I'd been spared a place like this when they had not. I also wondered, if Bob truly was innocent, to what purpose by God was he in such a place?

Juan was another surprise. Quiet so far, he went on for ten minutes about how grateful he was for his family, friends, faith, and relationship with God and Jesus. He thanked Jesus for working through the outsiders and bringing this REC to him. The pure joy and love on his face was remarkable and unforgettable.

Mary Fran read John 13:1-20 out loud:

> *It was just before the Passover Festival. Jesus knew that the hour had come for him to leave this world and go to the Father. Having loved his own who were in the world, he loved them to the end.*
>
> *The evening meal was in progress, and the devil had already prompted Judas, the son of Simon Iscariot, to betray Jesus. Jesus knew that the Father had put all things under his power, and that he had come from God and was returning to God; so, he got up from the meal, took off his outer clothing, and wrapped a towel around his waist. After that, he poured water into a basin and began to wash his disciples' feet, drying them with the towel that was wrapped around him.*

He came to Simon Peter, who said to him, "Lord, are you going to wash my feet?"

Jesus replied, "You do not realize now what I am doing, but later you will understand."

"No," said Peter, "you shall never wash my feet."

Jesus answered, "Unless I wash you, you have no part with me."

"Then, Lord," Simon Peter replied, "not just my feet but my hands and my head as well!"

Jesus answered, "Those who have had a bath need only to wash their feet; their whole body is clean. And you are clean, though not every one of you." For he knew who was going to betray him, and that was why he said not everyone was clean.

When he had finished washing their feet, he put on his clothes and returned to his place. "Do you understand what I have done for you?" he asked them. "You call me 'Teacher' and 'Lord,' and rightly so, for that is what I am. Now that I, your Lord and Teacher, have washed your feet, you also should wash one another's feet. I have set you an example that you should do as I have done for you. Very truly I tell you, no servant is greater than his master, nor is a messenger greater than the one who sent him. Now that you know these things, you will be blessed if you do them."

As she finished, the Wheaties brought out buckets of warm water, sponges, rags, and soap. The act of washing the feet of another and having one's feet washed is humbling, never degrading.

I sat on a stool, and beneath me a pair of feet that I swear could walk on water appeared. I didn't have to look up to know they were Jasper's. "I don't think there's enough soap for these boats."

When I finished, he leaned down and thanked me. All I could do was look up and acknowledge our friendship.

We finished and returned to our tables. Right on cue, we heard a chorus coming down the hall toward our sanctuary. Led by a priest, there were thirty people from the outside singing "What a Friend We Have in Jesus." They entered and walked around the room singing and greeted each resident with a smile and hug.

All Eight Disciples of Jesus grinned from ear to ear. They appreciated these new arrivals and understood a catered dinner was coming.

"What are we having, John?" asked Robert.

"Just wait!"

All RECs do some form of a hootenanny, but ours included additional outsiders and a meal with good conversation and mutual respect. The guards were edgy, but with more people in the room to protect and monitor, I didn't blame them.

"COUNT NOW!" yelled Harry.

He was not messing around, and the residents knew it. They leaped up and counted off before the words left Harry's mouth.

Once they'd sat back down, Olivia stood at the center of the room. "Quick prayer before we dive into barbecue ribs, chicken, and brisket. Our sides will be mashed potatoes, green beans, and a fresh salad. Croissants and a chocolate cake will be our baked goods. Please thank the providers from Potosi Barbecue for their donation as you are served."

Huge applause.

"Lord God and Giver of All Good Gifts, we are grateful as we pause before this meal for all the blessings of life that You give to us. Daily, we are fed with good things, nourished by friendship and care, feasted with forgiveness and understanding. And so, mindful of Your continuous care, we pause to be grateful for the blessings of this table. In Jesus name, we pray. Amen."

"Amen!"

It wasn't that long ago that I truly couldn't have cared less about my fellow human beings, but I have come a long way. You can't buy the joy I felt. These men appeared as happy as at almost any other time in their lives, yet they were still incarcerated. And it wasn't just the food, it was the fellowship and the whole REC experience.

But the food didn't hurt. I couldn't guess how many pounds of food Jasper put away.

Stuffed and sleepy, those who smoked took a break, and the chorus that delivered the provender bade their goodbyes and left to return to the outside world.

We cleaned, and Tony played his guitar, and then we settled back down at our tables.

"Our next talk," Olivia said, "will be from John at table six, *The Eight Disciples of Jesus.*"

In a low rumble at first, the voices of my table grew, "John, John, John . . ." as they stood and clapped.

I made my way to the kitchen, as was our tradition, where the Wheaties prayed with their hands laid upon me. "Jesus, help John our brother speak the truth, help him rise from the ashes. We pray he gets strength from you Lord. Bless his soul, save him from the destructiveness of Satan. Please let his audience be open to what he has to say. We pray in the strong and powerful blood of Jesus Christ, our Risen Savior and Lord. Amen."

"Amen," I repeated.

A robe was wrapped around my shoulders, and they led me to the front of the room behind the altar. There were only a few candles for light. Our little sanctuary was like a medieval church. I doubted again that I was up to the task.

"My name is John, and I'm an alcoholic."

"Hi, John," a handful of people replied.

I started the way I started every AA talk I've ever given. "I am grateful to be here and grateful to be sober. I am also grateful to be a recovering alcoholic.

"I would like to open with my favorite prayer and a prayer that I try to live by, The St. Francis Prayer:

> Lord, make me an instrument of your peace,
> Where there is hatred, let me sow love;
> where there is injury, pardon;
> where there is doubt, faith;
> where there is despair, hope;
> where there is darkness, light;
> where there is sadness, joy;
> O Divine Master, grant that I may not so much seek to be
>   consoled as to console;
> to be understood as to understand;
> to be loved as to love.
> For it is in giving that we receive;
> it is in pardoning that we are pardoned;
> and it is in dying that we are born to eternal life.
> Amen."

"Amen," came the reply.

"There are really two types of signs that I will describe for our purposes today. They are everyday visual signs such as traffic signs, sports signs, and audible signs, like a telephone tone or a church bell telling hours. These secular signs are used as a symbolic representation as opposed to written words. These signs are used to represent the existence of something. You must be listening or looking for these signs in your life.

"Then there are the seven Sacraments, which are the signs of God's love and presence in our life. The seven Sacraments are Baptism, Confession, Communion, Confirmation, Holy Matrimony, Holy Orders, and Anointing of the Sick. The Eucharist or Holy Communion is the most important of the seven.

"Jesus Christ established all seven of the Sacraments during his ministry, and they provide grace from the sacrificial death of Christ on the cross to the faithful throughout their lives, from birth to death. Reception of the Sacraments in accord with the teaching of the Church is the ordinary means of salvation for all the faithful.

"The seven sacraments have different meanings, or purposes. Baptism forgives all sins, takes away original sin. Confession forgives any sins committed after Baptism. Communion—The Holy Eucharist—is a sign of unity with other Catholics who are not aware of any unconfessed actual mortal sins. Confirmation calls upon members to profess faith in Christ publicly and to spread the Gospel message. Receiving this Sacrament, with Baptism and Communion, completes a person's initiation into the one Holy Catholic and Apostolic Church. Holy Matrimony is a Sacrament established by Jesus Christ for the benefit and salvation of the husband and wife and their children. It is a Holy bond before God. Holy Orders are the means by which Christ provides the faithful with true shepherds after his own heart. Anointing of the Sick is the last rites where the dying or extremely ill are offered forgiveness from sin, abundant grace, and healing in the body and soul.

"The Holy Eucharist or communion is the most important sign and is a sacrament and a sacrifice. In the Holy Eucharist, under the appearance of bread and wine, the Lord Christ is contained, offered, and received. Bread is a sign of Jesus's body, and wine is a sign of Jesus's blood. Understanding the Eucharist helps us understand God's love.

"There are many signs in mass from colors to dress to scripture readings to hymns to the Church and even the cross itself.

"For instance, the colors of a priest's vestments help the lay people understand what celebrations are at hand. Green signifies ordinary time and is the color of growth. Purple or violet is used during Advent and Lent and is the color of humility and penitence. White and gold are most appropriate during Christmas and Easter and signify baptism and life. The type of vestment also is a sign to people of the priest's position and standing in the church.

"Obviously, the sign of the cross has a very powerful meaning in the Catholic Church. To Christianity, the cross symbolizes redemption through the sacrificial death by crucifixion of Jesus Christ. It stands for suffering, triumph, and victory. The way to properly make the sign of the cross is to use your right hand and touch your forehead at the mention of the Father, the lower middle of your chest at the mention of the Son, your left shoulder on the word Holy, and your right shoulder on the word Spirit.

"Saying *amen* is an audible sign that means *So be it*. It is a sign that we are in agreement with Jesus Christ. It is a sign that we want to change so we can be more like Christ.

"The physical church is typically built in the shape of the cross for obvious reasons, and the spire or tower is designed to draw your eyes up to heaven. Christ is the head of the Church, and Christians are the body, whereas the actual church is the Bride of Christ, suggesting a family relationship between Christ and Church."

I paused and looked around the room. Their eyes were on me, but drifting. All I'd said so far was a mere lesson of history and ritual. There was no connection to my life or the residents' lives, nothing to connect any of us to the notion that God is seen through His signals of transcendence. Without a story behind it, all I'd said was just words.

"I should have noticed the signs of what was in store for me early in life. I lost all four of my grandparents when they were in their early sixties and I was under ten years of age. The funeral services were signs of loss. Not that I was aware at the time, but later in life, I heard they were all heavy drinkers and smokers except for my father's mother, Nana, who had polio at an early age. Sometimes signs can be subliminal and not make themselves apparent for many years, which was the case with my grandparents.

"I grew up in a family of abundance and material possessions, signs of success. We had a big house, expensive cars, private clubs and school. All the best money could offer. All signs to make our lives look good from the outside, but on the inside it was a disaster.

"I have very few memories of my mother, and those are not very fond memories. I asked my father recently why that was the case. He told me that Lizzy, my nanny, and he put my mother to bed very early in the evening, even before dinner, because she was so intoxicated.

"Maybe the frequent ambulance visits to our house when I was in high school should have been a sign that things were not normal. Maybe coming downstairs to find the Christmas tree had fallen over or that toys were not put together or a myriad of other things should have been signs of things to come. When you're young, you have very little control over what happens to you.

"At age nine, my parents sat us down in our perfectly decorated living room and told us they were getting divorced. I understood what that meant because a friend of mine's parents went through a divorce. My sister and brother were younger, six and three respectively, so they didn't really understand.

"My mother was sent away to treatment for alcoholism and didn't return for five years. During that time, we had a great life, just the five of us—Dad, Lizzy, my sister and brother, and me. We didn't understand that this was not a normal family and thought everything was perfectly okay.

"When my mother returned, it was with vengeance in her heart. She wanted vengeance against my father and against anyone she felt had wronged her. One path toward extracting as much pain as she could was suing for custody of my brother, sister, and me. My mother had an unlimited supply of money and constantly had my father in court. Eventually she won, and the judge awarded custody to her. Since I was fourteen, the judge allowed me to choose which parent I wanted to live with. I chose to abandon my brother and sister to my mother and live with my dad. I thought this would save me from living in a world of crazy drunks, but it didn't. What it did do was leave my sister and brother without anyone to protect them.

"My mother wasn't rehabilitated and had married another active alcoholic. You can imagine the turmoil that ensued. I remember the flashing lights and hearing the sirens approaching our house. All signs of very bad trouble. One time the medics were called to a restaurant we were dining in because my mother was choking on some food because she was too intoxicated to swallow.

"We were all verbally abused by my mother and stepfather. My brother was physically abused by our stepfather. And then at age twenty-two, when I was in college, my mother fell for the last time and hit her head on the fireplace. She remained in a coma for five days until it was decided to pull the plug. All the tubes and equipment were signs the end was near. There were no tears.

"This was not a sad time.

"At one time, my mother was a gorgeous, very intelligent socialite with literally hundreds of friends. When she married my father, there were twenty showers held in her honor prior to the wedding.

"In attendance at the funeral were my aunt, my stepfather, my brother, my sister, and me. A very strong sign of where her life of addiction led her.

"You would think that I would have picked up on this rather obvious sign, but my drinking started in my teens and just escalated from there. I was never a social drinker. I drank to kill pain and fill a God-sized hole. And you know what? It worked well for a while.

"There were not a lot of consequences early on, but I did receive the signs audibly from my girlfriend and stepmother. My father remarried just before my mother came back, which made for a lot of change over a few months. Both parents remarrying and bringing someone new into my life that I didn't know, understand, or really want any part of. I was happy with dad, Lizzy, my sister, and my brother.

"On many occasions, my girlfriend broke up with me because of my drinking and wandering ways. I got the drinking talk early on from my stepmother who warned me I was becoming my mother.

"Within a few months of my mother's passing, my uncle, my father's brother, passed away. I loved Uncle Mike, and he was always there for us, especially when Dad was divorced and trying to raise the three of us. He would come by early Saturday mornings and take us for the day to give Lizzy and Dad a break. No one spoke much about his passing, but it was due to his drinking as well.

"My father took over my grandfather's successful shoe business when he was fairly young. At one point, he had to fire his own brother because of Uncle Mike's drinking and inability to quit.

"I remember exactly where I was standing when I made the declaration that I would never become an alcoholic like my mother. Do you think I listened to any of these signs of what was in store for me? Of course not. I had to suffer through the pain of addiction for the next twenty years and all the consequences that come with the disease.

"I muddled along through life with my alcoholism progressing and married when I was thirty. Just prior to my wedding, I received my first of what would be three arrests for driving while intoxicated. I wasn't a little over the limit. I was so beyond the limit that I was lucky I didn't have to be hospitalized for alcohol poisoning after all three arrests. What a sign, but it didn't slow me down one iota.

"I was living in Texas at the time, and pretty soon after we were married, my wife and I had a beautiful little girl. I loved her to death, but it wasn't enough to slow my drinking down. We decided to move back to St. Louis where we had another child, a boy this time whom I adored.

"I started a hidden dog fence business in St. Louis that enabled me to drink throughout the day, and eventually I got involved in an alcoholic affair.

"Three DWIs, a divorce, a car repossessed, house close to foreclosure, loss of children, business almost closed, hadn't filed with the IRS in three years, no money, family and friends long gone, a false child abuse charge, a harassment charge, and on and on. My life was a mess, and all the signs were there to prove it, yet I kept going, thinking I was on top of the world.

"That is what addiction does to you. All that grandiosity, and I was almost as far down as you could go. I remember driving blind drunk a few days before my life disintegrated, thinking that I had a great life.

"What a joke!

"By the time I checked into treatment, I was close to death, and the doctor had to make an emergency call to my primary physician to find out what drugs I could take because I was close to having a heart attack or stroke.

"All the signs were there, but I ignored every single one of them and in the process hurt many, many people, including myself. Most of all, I hurt my innocent children whom I have no relationship with today even though I have years of sobriety and made direct amends to them and their mother. By far and away, this is the saddest part of my story and one that will haunt me to my grave.

"The biggest sign I have of how far my disease took me is the night I backed my car down the driveway to go to my alcoholic lover. I looked up to see my two darling children waving goodbye to me. That image haunts me and still brings tears to my eyes.

"Maybe having to chug warm beer at five or five-thirty in the morning to stop the shakes and feel halfway normal was a sign. Or drinking around the clock was a sign that there were problems.

"Obviously, I am a very slow learner and have to take as much pain as humanly possible before finally succumbing.

"The signs were all there. I failed to notice them along the way or maybe just denied their existence and felt as though I was invincible. Even if God had hit me over the head with any kind of sign at that point in my life, I probably wouldn't have noticed.

"God didn't leave me. I left him. He provided all the signs I needed to know I was in trouble. I chose to ignore those signs.

"The amount of loss in my life, mostly due to the disease of addiction, is staggering. All I can do is hope that I have stopped the cycle and future generations of my family won't have to suffer the way I and many relatives before me have. I would like to be the last generation of alcoholics in my family.

"Today I look for those signs. If a sign says stop, I stop. If it says yield, I am patient and wait my turn. What an easier, softer way of life I have discovered. If I am aware and vigilant of warning signs, my life turns out well. It took me a long time to understand that, but today I am a recovering alcoholic, and I am thankful to God every day.

"Without going through all the pain, I wouldn't have changed. It took every drink and drug to get me into the program of Alcoholics Anonymous and keep me here.

"To be one hundred percent truthful, the main reason I stay sober is that I have too much fear to go back. My counselors have told me the disease is progressive, and I have witnessed that in others who decided to test the waters. I believe that with all my heart. I also believe that I didn't leave any space before death for the disease to progress, should I start to drink again. The next drink or drug for me is death, and I assure each one of you I have way too good of a life and too much left to do to leave the planet right now.

"I have an amazing life today, but I have to stay centered and balanced to maintain my serenity. I go to a minimum of one AA meeting per day, I pray on my knees in the morning and thank God before I go to sleep. Before I fall asleep, I take a daily inventory to check and make sure there wasn't anything I need to apologize for or that I could do better. I try to help other alcoholics and sponsor men in AA. At this point, the twelve steps work me, but I revisit them often.

"I am starting to get a little better at meditating, but it is difficult for me to sit still for any length of time. I talk with four or five recovering alcoholics a day. If I have a big decision to make, I run it by my sponsor first and then I have a small committee of men I run things by. My best thinking got me in the mess I was in, so I need help seeing what is and isn't true before acting on an idea.

"I work on my character defects, which are very difficult to change. The biggest being impatience, which I struggle with daily. I am also very judgmental, self-centered, and opinionated.

"The most important thing today is that I am aware of my character defects as is my sponsor. If I get off course, I notice it, or he notices it, and I can adjust. I am nowhere near perfect, but I am slowly becoming the person I believe God meant for me to be.

"I believe God's will for me is to stay sober and help other people, not just alcoholics. My sober pathway is to be of service to anyone who needs my help. That is the motto I try to live by today. For so many years, I was a taker. I was an egomaniac with an inferiority complex. I didn't care about anybody or anything if I got what I wanted. I was a liar, adulterer, thief, con artist and much, much more.

"Today, I am an example of AA and what it can do for people all over the world. As soon as I walk out the doors of an AA meeting, I might be the only person a normal person has an interaction with, and I want that interaction to be the most positive possible.

"There are too many negative connotations associated with AA. We are a cult, it doesn't work, etcetera, etcetera. I am living proof that it does work and works very well. Now, granted only five to ten percent of the newcomers to AA maintain sobriety for a year, but it is better than anything else I've ever tried. It is simply one person reaching out to another person.

"Someone asked me a while back if I could describe in a few words how to get sober.

"That's an easy one, and it will only take one word.

"Change.

"The next three words are change, change, and change.

"Sounds simple, but it is almost impossible for a person to change and stay changed. That's where the old phrase *a leopard never changes its spots* comes from.

"There are other ways to become sober and live a sober life, but I can only speak from my experience. I have a sponsor, a counselor, I am involved with Native American sweat lodges, I pray, meditate, read, work the twelve steps, and a few more things. It takes a lot of help from the outside to help this sick man to get better, and today I am not afraid to ask for help. A huge change, I assure you.

"It will take the rest of my life to correct my actions, and I will probably never get there, but today I am at least willing to try and pray for forgiveness for my past immoral behavior.

"When I came through the doors of AA, I wasn't looking for a spiritual awakening or a relationship with a higher power, but that is exactly what I got and much more. All my friends and family— except for my children—are back in my life. I have made amends to most of those I have hurt. I have financially climbed out of the hole I created and am now headed in the other direction. I repaid and replaced all that I took and stole.

"I even read the letter of forgiveness I wrote to my mother over her grave. Today I truly understand that she did the best she could do. That was extremely difficult for me to believe, but with the help of God, I got there.

"I leave this part of my story for last because I never want to forget how it ends or that I have a long way still to go. I have no relationship with my children. They really want nothing to do with me. They moved to Dallas, so I only see them a few times a year when I go there. They refuse to come to St. Louis to see me or their family here. I pray that this changes at some point in the future, but without a doubt, this is the saddest part of my story and where I caused the most damage.

"How could I have possibly hurt those two innocent little children?

"This was a consequence of my drinking, and I will have to live with that for the rest of my life. The continuing nightmare of my two children waving goodbye to me from the dining room window while I go to drink and mess around with another woman. How pathetic!

"All I can do is try to be the best father possible from this day forward and pray to God that He will help me with my relationship with my children and repair the damaged I caused.

"I thank God I am a sober alcoholic today. Thank you, and God bless you and this correctional facility."

Tears streamed down my face. *How could that be enough?*

###

The residents stood and applauded. There were shouts of "John. John, John . . ." and someone called out, "Praise the Lord, he has spoken through John."

I felt I didn't deserve it. All I did was tell my story.

As I made my way back to the table, my hands trembled, my chest felt tight, and I was a bit lightheaded. Then Manuel grabbed me around my shoulders. "So good, John, thank you," he said while giving me a little shake.

I wiped the tears from my eyes and face with the back of one hand, and Leroy patted my shoulder. "That was good, really good," he whispered.

The men at the other tables continued to applaud, and I looked around at them, their eyes on me, and I felt humbled and embarrassed. *Who am I to receive so much from these folks?* I wondered.

At the same time, I felt good. I gave all that I had, and it seemed to be enough. A few more of the Eight Disciples of Jesus hugged me and in one form or another thanked me for my story. Maybe by being so open and transparent before them, they'd come to believe that they shouldn't be afraid of their own stories.

Or maybe not. I didn't know, but my feelings of self-doubt gave way to an inner warmth that I would describe as a modest elation. It wasn't that I'd won anything or proved myself more adept than another. It was more a sense of belonging to these people and this mission because of what I had brought to it rather than because I was an alcoholic in recovery.

I guess it's a difficult feeling to describe. God took me in because I am a child of His. AA took me in because I not only needed them, but I wanted them. To the people I'd sponsored, I was a friend, but also a means to an end. But here, in this death row REC, these men didn't need me. I had no pardons to pass out. They were not beholden to me in any way. And yet they accepted me and found value in what I had to say to them. It wasn't a sales job on my part. I transparently shared who I am and what I'd learned from a lifetime's worth of guilt and shame.

I looked up and thanked God.

Things quieted down, and we sat at our table to discuss what I'd said. There was no way not to notice Jasper. Tears glistened against his skin, and the whites of his eyes were red.

"What's wrong, Jasper?" I asked.

"Man, you got the saddest story I ever heard."

This statement seemed so far out that I had a hard time comprehending the meaning, much less how to respond. In a few hours, I'd leave this place to sleep in a hotel room, and the next day I would return home to a life he likely would never have. For good reason, I didn't ask any of the men if they were in for life or faced execution, but how could Jasper say such a thing, knowing his fate? How could I, John Lipscomb, have the saddest story Jasper ever heard? Was there something I had missed? He was either mistaken or didn't know me well enough.

I looked to the other Disciples of Jesus, and they nodded their heads. Was it in agreement or just in support of Jasper, a man whose fate they were well aware of?

I would like to say that I had the perfect response. One of grace, modesty, and honesty that laid bare some compassionate and hopeful truth. Instead, tears streamed down my face.

"What?" I asked.

"You got the saddest story I ever heard."

Maybe Jasper did know something I didn't. Maybe he understood the prison addiction and bad choices had put me in for most of my life. Maybe Jasper could feel the same losses I felt. Maybe God was working within Jasper to help him understand that grace is there for those who want it. Maybe he was saying the sadness, pain, and fear were lifted, and he saw a path toward having a life worth living. Rather than dim outlines and hope, it was now real to him.

"You do understand that I am leaving here in a few hours and you are not?" I asked.

"Yes."

"You realize that I'll sleep in a warm bed and have good food soon?"

"Yes."

"Then how in the world can you say that I have the saddest story you ever heard?"

"For me and most of us in here, our lives were predictable and known well before we arrived here. We were almost raised in the system, so nothing that happened to us was a surprise. We have food, shelter, friends, and some have family. There's TV, exercise, and besides the occasional scuffles, we are safe from the streets."

The other Disciples nodded.

"Look at your life, John. You started out at the top, and by the end of your story, you are leaning over the edge, eyes staring into the abyss with nowhere to turn. You hit bottom hard. Look at your losses—your mom, wife, two children, uncle, grandparents, friends, all these people in your life, gone.

"They were dead to you, and you were dead to them. What was left for you to live for? And yet somehow you stepped back from the brink."

"Whoa, whoa, I didn't do anything. It was God who pulled me out. I don't take any credit for it. If it had been up to me, I'd be dead."

"God has saved all of us from ourselves. I see that now, clearly, but it is much harder to be on top of the mountain and fall than it is to start at the bottom and look up. We knew what to expect and were told by many people in many ways what to expect from life. It was often bleak tempered by some hope, but it was predictable. You fell and went to places you never could have expected in ways you never could have known.

"We all had a tremendous amount of loss, and the world I grew up in, probably all of us here grew up in, was scary, but it was expected. When you hit bottom, you had to change your life from your heart and soul all the way out.

"It's a sad story, John. We all have sad stories, but yours is the saddest I've heard."

I was touched and got up and hugged Jasper. He hugged me back, and I felt as if I disappeared into him, but I still didn't understand what he was saying. How could I?

"COUNT!" screamed Harry, the guard.

We went through the Saturday liturgy and then Terry, our spiritual director, read a story called "Ragman" while a handful of insiders and outsiders acted out the various characters and scenes.

After the story ended, Harry stepped forward. "LINE UP! TIME TO CALL IT A NIGHT!"

About thirty minutes later, we stepped out into the cool early spring air. The others breathed in deeply and chatted, but I was lost in thought.

"What's wrong, Johnny?" Olivia asked.

I was weeping lightly and thankful for the darkness. "Just something Jasper said."

"What?"

"He told me I had the saddest story he ever heard."

"Gosh."

"Do I?"

"Who knows, Johnny. Everyone has a story, and whether yours is the saddest is up to that person. Maybe it is in Jasper's eyes."

I turned to her and sobbed on her shoulder. For the life of me, I had no idea why I was crying. Relief, exhaustion, the truth of my life hitting me all at once? But it was cleansing.

The next day we all received letters written to us from a person—outsider or insider—in the REC. Of course, mine was from Jasper:

> *John,*
>
> *God bless you. You have been funny and kindhearted. Please continue to serve God and to be a servant. I feel blessed to meet someone as nice and wonderful as you.*
>
> *Your friend in Jesus,*
>
> *Jasper*

I should stop all this crying was all I could think. I peered over at Jasper and winked in acknowledgment.

The Wheaties passed out a snack, and the men dug into it, though there was a greater sense of calm. Faith blanketed them. I could see it in their eyes, and in that moment, I knew that this state of faith, respect, and serenity is what God intends for us. I am fortunate to have witnessed what true faith can do for people. It is an amazing and spiritual sensation that I have experienced during sweat lodges, AA, and on death row. It is more addictive than any substance on earth, and I wish I could bottle it and drink when life throws me off balance or pass it along to others in need of a spiritual awakening. But really, it is available to all. The signals of God and His love are here if we look for them.

Looking at the men of Potosi, it was as if they were untouchable. God and their desire to be close to Him and Jesus made this possible.

Later in the day, after lunch as we smoked, I got the chance to speak with Harry. "What do you think?"

"I don't really know. I'm not a believer, but the transformation in these guys over the weekend is staggering. I have been here a long time, and the RECs do seem to have a calming effect both in your sanctuary and the yard. For some, it lasts a while, and others revert to their old ways pretty quickly."

"Just like on the outside. I believe it's almost impossible to change permanently unless it is truly a life or death situation. Most people have the capability to change for brief periods, but generally it doesn't last.

"Now, if these guys can fake it until they make it, you know, stick with it for a little while, change is possible. Like any good habit, if you keep repeating it over and over, it eventually becomes part of you."

Harry nodded. "I just wish it would stick with these guys longer. It would sure make my life easier. What you're doing is commendable. Why you're doing it, I have no idea. Even their family and friends don't waste their time on many of them."

"Truth is, I do it more for me than anything else. I love helping them, but it's part of my program of sobriety."

He smiled. "I hope it continues to work for you, I really do." Then he called out that it was time to go back to the REC.

As we walked, a few of the men joked or chatted. I wondered if Harry would be one of the men leading them to the execution chamber. Probably not, but he must see them as they are led away and taken to the cell just outside of the death chamber in preparation for their execution. He must also feel their absence when they are gone. How could he not?

"I hope the next few hours go well," Harry said as we entered our sanctuary.

"Thanks for your help, Harry. I hope you get something out of this as well."

The remainder of the day included the commitment service, Sunday liturgy, Eucharist, and the presentation of pictures, cards, and crosses.

When we reached the Eucharist, each table made its way to the altar. The mood was solemn, and I could hear the priest say, "Take this, for this is the body of Christ, and drink this for it is the blood of Christ."

After the last person received communion, Olivia stepped to the center of the room and said it was time to hand out the photos and crosses.

Tears streamed from my eyes when I handed each his photos and card and placed the cross around his neck. Jasper was last, and I couldn't look him in the eyes. I was a mess. He leaned forward and with deliberate ease, I hung the cross from him. There were tears in his eyes, too.

"LINE UP!" Harry shouted.

The outsiders lined up on both sides of the doorway. The residents started to make their way out, back into the world of prison and death row. There wasn't a dry eye, including the guards. Jesus and God were in this room, at least for the weekend.

I grabbed Jasper's hand as he passed. "You'll never know what your friendship means to me, brother. When you read your card, please know that I mean every word. Go in peace, and I look forward to seeing you at the reunion."

His smile was bittersweet. "John, thank you for being a friend, brother, and mentor. God bless you and your angels, as you refer to the people here."

In silence, we took down our banners and returned the room to its normal state.

I sat next to Olivia as we rode in a van from Potosi.

"Well, what did you think?" she asked.

"It was an amazing experience. I can't thank you enough for including me."

"I noticed you became particularly close to Jasper. What did you write in his card?"

"I told Jasper that I thanked God He put him in my life. Remember I told you he said I had the saddest story he ever heard?"

"Yes."

"Well, I explained to him that although I appreciated his thoughts, I didn't personally believe my story was so sad and that I wasn't looking for pity or sorrow. It was simply my story."

"Very good. You're growing up quickly, Johnny Lipscomb. I hope you continue on your path of helping others and helping yourself by doing so."

I drove home in silence, no music, top up. When I entered my home, I burst into tears thinking about how sad my life was. All the losses, all the chaos I created, all the people I hurt. I realized it would take a lifetime of doing the right thing to set it better. Some of the sadness was beyond my control, but because of my addiction and selfishness, I had caused a lot of pain.

AFTERWORD

I DIDN'T DO MUCH for the few days after the REC. I thought and thought about the weekend and all that transpired. Eventually, I made it back into the real world and continued with my regular routines.

The month passed quickly, and I was ready to see the residents and our team members from the REC at our reunion. I'd come to love these reunions. They were happy occasions, even if fewer residents chose to attend, and they offered a sense of closure, of completeness.

We entered Potosi and made our way through the airlocks and into the yard and then to our sanctuary. It was just a big bland room.

I'd gotten used to the fact that during a REC I may get close to the people at my table and some others, but that didn't mean I would see them at the reunion. It was always a surprise to see who came back and could remain close to God and seek out a better, fuller life. But I did expect that I would see Jasper. How could I not?

We heard the residents approach and got in line to greet them. Tony got us started with "Go Tell It on The Mountain," and we heard the residents joining in from the other side of the door as they made their way toward us.

They all but burst through the doorway and were greeted with hugs and smiles. Though there were half as many as at the REC, they greeted us with warmth and joy in their hearts.

I looked around for my tablemates and quickly found Juan, Bob, and Leroy.

"Where's Jasper?" I asked.

Juan looked toward the floor then back to me. "I have no idea where that guy is."

Harry stood by the door. I looked toward him. He turned his eyes from mine.

AUTHOR'S NOTE

First and foremost, I have to thank the Angels of the REC (Residents Encounter Christ) program.

That includes The Catholic Church, inside and outside participants, volunteers, the wardens of the prisons where I participated, the guards, those who wrote Palanca letters, and certainly all of those who prayed before, during, and after the RECs for us. I have to also thank those who donated time, money, and catered food. Without all of those mentioned above, the REC program just wouldn't be possible. So thank you from the bottom of my heart.

The actual crimes were not disclosed, nor were my views on capital punishment, on purpose. They are irrelevant to my story. All names were changed to protect those who did not wish to have their names known publicly.

I also need to state that I was baptized Episcopal, and in my thirties I became a Methodist. I am not an overly religious man but believe in God and Jesus. The welcoming Catholic Church is how I was granted access to the prisons. Because of the graciousness of the Catholic Church, people from other religious faiths are accepted into the REC program as well. Through interviews, my memory, others' memories, and research, I believe I have come as close as humanly possible to the correct terminology and events that transpire during a REC weekend.

Because of the immense interest in my co-authored first book, *The Painting and The Piano,* I was asked numerous times to expand on some of the things I have done in the past few years.

Inevitably the work that I did with prisoners came up, and once I started telling the story of Jasper, eyes got wide, chins dropped, mouths went wide open, and without exception, each person listened to the tiniest detail without speaking. That's when I knew I had a story worth telling. The words poured out of me in a very few months, and the one-hundred-percent factual story of Jasper was born.

I want to be perfectly clear and honest that I do not personally believe I have the saddest story, and I am not looking for a pity party. In fact, it is quite the opposite. I believe I have had a great life with many advantages that others simply did not have, and I am one of the luckiest individuals on the planet. I wouldn't change my life with anyone.

I need to thank my incredible team, which includes Adrianne, Olivia, James, and Laurie. Without their help and encouragement, this story would have been lost in the depths of time.

Thank you so much to my readers for your continued support!